CENTRAL OREGON WILDERNESS AREAS

(Cascades to the Coast)

by
Donna Ikenberry Aitkenhead

Photographs by
Donna and Roger Aitkenhead

The Touchstone Press
P.O. Box 81
Beaverton, Oregon 97075

Additional Touchstone Press books by Donna Aitkenhead

SOUTHERN OREGON WILDERNESS AREAS
EASTERN OREGON WILDERNESS AREAS

*For my parents, Beverly and Donald Ikenberry,
and my brothers Don and Dave Ikenberry.*

*I thank God for you each day and am
so proud to be a part of our family.*

Patjens Lake and Mt. Washington

CENTRAL OREGON WILDERNESS AREAS

CONTENTS

Mink Lake at sunrise

CENTRAL OREGON WILDERNESS AREAS

INTRODUCTION

I've sat for the longest time, trying to describe the multi-faceted Central Oregon area in one word and I just can't do it. How can a single word accurately describe this scenic wonderland? Should I say it is lush? Well, yes, that describes a lot of the region, but not all of it. The jagged peaks, glaciers, and lava flows in some of the areas are mind-boggling, but certainly not lush.

Does the word "beautiful" characterize the region? Of course it does, but so does stunning, amazing, awesome, startling, and a hundred other terms. I guess if I'm to begin this introduction I'll have to use the word "diversity," and you'll find plenty of that in Central Oregon's Wilderness Areas.

In the Beaver State, there are more than two million acres of designated wilderness managed as such in 37 individual areas. (One wilderness, the nation's smallest and least accessible, bobs off the Oregon coast. Oregon Islands is only 485 acres and consists of 56 islands/groups.) The eight preserves listed in this guidebook total 456,480 acres, about one-fifth of the state total. Each is different from the other, most with individual characteristics of their own.

For instance, the Waldo Lake Wilderness is more than a forest covering steep slopes and rugged canyons. It's a land of old-growth forest where ancient 800-year-old western red cedar trees grow along a white-water river. Cold streams gush down mountainsides, flowing into crystal-clear Waldo Lake. Atop prominent peaks, one can "see forever," observing Mt. Hood and other Cascade peaks in the distance. Yes, Waldo Lake Wilderness and the other preserves listed in this book are filled with variety.

The Three Sisters, Oregon's second largest wilderness and the most visited, contains tall snow-capped peaks. Glaciers flank the sides of some of the highest summits. Hikers stroll through flower-filled meadows, lava fields, dense forest, into deep valleys and past hundreds of clear blue lakes.

All the preserves provide something unique and special. In the Menagerie Wilderness, rock climbers come to test their skills, climbing 300-foot pinnacles. The three coastal areas, Rock Creek, Drift Creek and Cummins Creek, provide little in the way of trails, but plenty of opportunities for bushwhacking through splendid stands of old-growth. Diamond Peak offers wide vistas, quiet lakes, and the chance to bag another high mountain peak. In the Mount Washington area, hikers pass through immense lava fields, signature cards from a time long ago.

By now you may be wondering, "What is wilderness?"

Although there are many definitions of it (to some it may be playing in a congested mountain stream), wilderness as defined in this book is subject to those areas designated by Congress. President Lyndon Johnson signed the Wilderness Act into effect on September 3, 1964.

Throughout the United States, there are over ninety-one million acres of wilderness (at 474 locations) administered under the National Wilderness Preservation System. This all-important law states that wilderness "shall be administered for the use and enjoyment of the American people in such a manner as will leave them unimpaired for future use and enjoyment as wilderness, and so as to provide for the protection of these areas (and) the preservation of their wilderness character."

Today, "wilderness character" is becoming more and more difficult to protect. Why? Because, we are loving this fragile ecosystem to death. Many areas suffer due to overcrowding. Like herd animals, some folks tend to flock together. We need to spread out. Instead of traveling familiar trails, why not explore someplace new?

Overcrowding in the Three Sisters and Mt. Washington areas prompted hearings in August, 1989, with the Forest Service trying to determine what should be done to prevent further degradation.

One solution is to limit access. Some national forests have already adopted such a plan. The Wenatchee National Forest in Washington, for example, adopted a permit system to keep down foot traffic in the Alpine Lakes Wilderness. Before reaching a solution, up to 300 campers would crowd into the Enchantment Lakes Basin. Now, 60 persons at a time are allowed in.

I must admit that we to are guilty of visiting some areas that collect more use than we'd like. Most of the time, however, we've searched for trails that receive little use. Whenever possible, we've refrained from visiting overcrowded and overused areas.We tried to find those places that provide a "true wilderness experience."

According to the law, wilderness is managed for its pristine character. True wilderness, the one for which all of us strive for, is a place where one can experience risk, charm, and isolation. It's a place "where man is a visitor who does not remain," and a place where certain rules apply. People of all ages must learn the "No Trace" concept, for if we fail to do so, the wilderness will perish. Everyone should learn to "Take only pictures; leave only footprints."

Often a hike through a flower-filled meadow, will tempt some folks to pick a few of the delicate blossoms. Please don't! If you want to remember this special moment, take a photograph. It'll last a lot longer than a flower that will soon wither and die. Best of all, it'll find a special place in the pages of your mind's own memory book.

The same policy applies to artifacts. Please look at them, take pictures if you will, then leave them alone.

Now that we've discussed taking pictures, you'll want to know about leaving footprints. Hikers should leave footprints on the trails, not off to the side of the trail. If you come across a muddy trail, plow right through. Detouring around a soggy portion increases the damage by creating another trail. In some areas, two or more unsightly trails lead side-by-side to a particular destination.

When switchbacking up or down a slope, please remain on the trail. Ugly shortcuts lead to erosion. If traveling cross-country, especially if in a group, do not walk one behind the other. Spread out. Hikers ambling across tundra or meadows can smash plant tissue beyond recovery and create channels for erosion.

When darkness is upon you, and you're ready to choose a campsite, please choose one wisely. Pick a site previously used instead of crushing untouched vegetation. Avoid camping in meadows, or along fragile lakeshores and stream banks. Why not pitch a tent or throw out your sleeping bag on a ridgetop? Often breezy, but fewer bugs frequent these areas.

While some management plans call for campsites more than 100 feet from water, some areas require choosing a site a minimum of 200 feet from a water source. Check with the Forest Service managing the area you plan to visit for more details.

When it comes to cooking (the time of day many backpackers like best) you'll have to use a camp stove or build a fire. The majority of backcountry users prefer a small, portable camp stove as they leave no trace whatsoever. They are efficient, lightweight, and easy to use. Those who would rather build a campfire should do so only when dead wood is available on the ground. And all fires should be completely out before leaving the campsite. In some areas there are restrictions regarding campfires. Please check with the managing Forest for up-to-date information.

Always pack out your garbage; never bury it. Wild animals may dig it up. (Also, do not feed the wildlife.) If you burn your trash, remember cans and foil do not burn. Please pack out what you pack in. Often, we see beverage cans or bottles, candy wrappers, and orange peels on the trail. There is absolutely no excuse for this behavior. The contents, already consumed, make trash light and easy to carry out.

When bathing or washing your clothes, please do so away from any water source including streams, springs, and lakes. Use all soaps, including biodegradable, and toothpaste at least 100 feet away from water and always bury your toothpaste.

Use the "cat method" to dispose of human waste. For those unfamiliar with this technique, dig a hole six to eight inches deep, placing the top soil to one side. (A light garden trowel works well.) After use, plug the hole with loose soil then stamp in the top soil. Before leaving, cover with a rock if possible.

Primitive methods of travel are suitable for trips into the wilderness. These include backpacking, day hiking, or riding a horse. Other methods of travel include bringing along a pack animal such as a horse, mule, or llama. Or, you may want to bring along a backpacking dog like we do.

Mechanical or motorized methods of travel, including motorcycles and mountain bikes, are prohibited and incompatible with wilderness travel.

Bringing dogs into the wilderness is often a subject of controversy. Should they, or should they not be allowed? I understand there are those who object to dogs in the wilderness, but there are also those who'd choose them over people. More than one person says, "Well, at least dogs do not litter or throw beer cans on the trail." Still others claim that dogs bark and chase wildlife.

Keep your *leashed* pet quiet and under control, and there should be no problem at all. Those that do not want to leash their pets or keep them quiet, should leave their animals at home.

Besides dogs on the trail, hikers may share it with horseback riders, too. Please note, those on horseback have the right of way and hikers should move to the down side of the trail when meeting riders.

Horseback riders please note, there's a limit of 10 or 12 persons/animal groups allowed in the wilderness. For example, you may have a group of six people and six pack animals, or nine people and three pack animals. Picket animals at least 200 feet from any water source, and carry feed for your animals.

Do you come to the wilderness with hunting or fishing on your mind? If so, please check with the agency managing the wilderness you are interested in to purchase permits and obtain up-to-date information on opening and closing dates.

While traveling throughout the preserves you may think that the springs, streams and rivers you pass are clear and pure. Clear they may be, but often they are far from pure. Unfortunately Giardia lamblia, a parasite, plagues some of the waters causing "backpackers' diarrhea" in some folks.

Hikers should be cautious of all water sources, even if it feels cold, looks pure, smells clean, and tastes fine. And if your hiking buddy picks up the dreaded parasite, you may find comfort in knowing that while one person may pick up the "bug," the other (even though he or she drank from the same source) may show no symptoms whatsoever. Those touched by Giardia may suffer from diarrhea, loss of appetite, abdominal cramps, gas and bloating.

What can you do to prevent "backpacker's diarrhea?" First, boil all water. Experts disagree on boiling time. Some claim boiling water a minimum of one minute at altitudes below 4,000 feet should do the trick. At higher altitudes boil water for a longer period. Still others recommend boiling all water for 10 minutes, regardless of the altitude. There are several other methods of treating water. These include water purifiers and commercial water purification chemicals. Please note, these are not always effective in killing the organisms.

I'm sure you've had enough of wilderness rules. Why not go ahead and plan your next hiking trip? Where will you go? What will you do? Whatever you decide, please follow the above suggestions. By doing so, you'll insure a "true wilderness experience" for future generations.

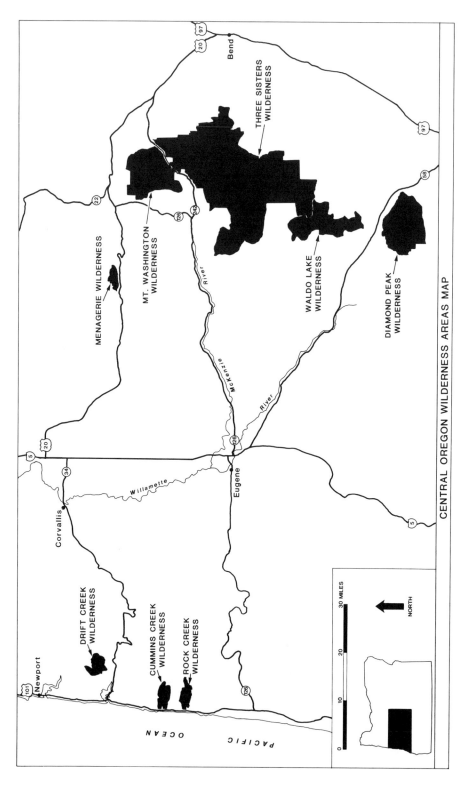

CENTRAL OREGON WILDERNESS AREAS MAP

CENTRAL OREGON WILDERNESS AREAS

INTRODUCTION TO THE CUMMINS CREEK WILDERNESS

Dense rain forest and solitude combine to make the Cummins Creek Wilderness a special place to visit. See the finest example of Sitka spruce trees, and enjoy a day of peace and quiet. Be prepared, however, to hike along an old road, as maintained trails are nonexistent and the thick vegetation makes cross-country travel nearly impossible.

This region is often difficult to explore for dense undergrowth prevails. Look for light pink rhododendron blooms in May. Other plant species include salal, sword fern and salmonberry. Watch for red alder, bigleaf maple, and vine maple lining the creeks. Wildflowers (including yellow monkeyflowers, purple asters and delicate candyflowers), often enchant spring visitors. In addition, there are red foxglove and lily-of-the-valley.

Ringed by roads, the 26 square mile preserve lies about 15 miles north of Florence and 5 miles south of Waldport. Established in 1984 with the signing of the Oregon Wilderness Act, the 9,278 acre preserve is managed by the Siuslaw National Forest.

The Forest Service allows hikers into the area but it does not allow horses. The fragile soil is not compatible with horse travel.

Elevation ranges from 100 feet near the Pacific Ocean to 2400 feet close to Cummins Peak. Two principal streams—Cummins Creek and Bob Creek—drain into the Pacific. Both support significant runs of anadromous fish.

Anglers should note that the Forest Service claims the fishing isn't very good in Cummins Creek, but it is a good spawning area.

Sixty to eighty inches of rain fall upon this land of steep valleys, Sitka spruce, hemlock, and Douglas fir. In the summer, chilly fogs envelop the coast and nearby valleys. Winters are usually free of snow. While year-round access is possible, fall and spring are the best times to visit for there's a better chance of clear skies.

Wildlife abounds in the region. The controversial spotted owl nests here as well as other owl and bird species. Animals making their home here include Roosevelt elk, black-tailed deer and black bear.

Two trails begin at the Cummins Ridge Trailhead. The only wilderness trail (an abandoned road) continues east from the trailhead, traveling 3.0 miles along the ridgetop. An unofficial trail heads north from the barricade, just outside the wilderness boundary. The unmaintained spur road is not suitable for vehicles. Keep left on this spur for less than a half mile to a scenic bench of old-growth Sitka spruce.

Two new trails should pop up in the future. The Forest Service plans to link the trail on Cummins Ridge with an old trail near Cummins Peak. Another trail will link the Cummins Basin Trail with the Cummins Ridge Trail, tying in with the Cape Perpetua Trail System.

For more information contact:

Forest Supervisor
Waldport Ranger District
P.O. Box 400
Waldport, OR 97394
(503) 563-3211

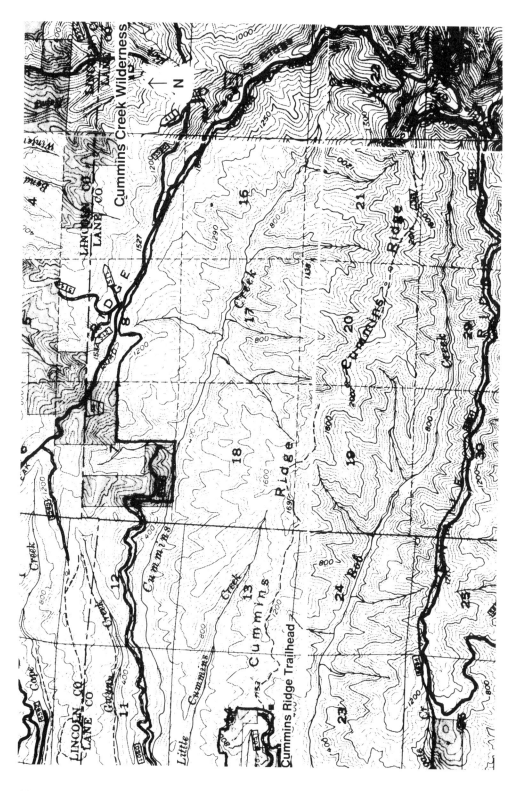

1 CUMMINS RIDGE TRAIL

Distance: 2.9 miles (one-way)
Elevation gain: 740 feet; loss 20 feet
High point: 1600 feet
Usually open: Year-round
Topographic map: U.S.G.S. Waldport,
Oregon, and U.S.G.S.
Heceta Head, Oregon
Obtain map from: U.S.G.S.—Denver, CO.

Cummins Creek Wilderness is a land where getting around isn't easy. The vegetation is nearly impenetrable, steep and rugged. Hikers prefer using trails when possible.

Well, you won't find standard trails in this Wilderness, but you will find an old road that's a welcome relief for those who'd like a peek into this little-used area.

To reach the trailhead for Cummins Ridge, drive 4.6 miles south from Yachats via U.S. Hwy. 101. You'll find gas, food and accommodations in this small coastal town. From the main highway, turn east onto FS Road No. 1051 and drive 2.2 miles to the trailhead.

The Cummins Ridge Trail consists of an old logging road. Today this is covered with grass, and other vegetation is slowly making a comeback. Notice the sweet smells of the forest, hear birds singing, and look for elk and bear scat of which we saw plenty. Also look for claw marks scratched in the trees by the local bears.

The trail heads up at a moderate grade then descends some before reaching the end of the road at 2.9 miles. Before the trail ends, look for a trail leading off to the left. For a good view of the Wilderness, take this trail for several hundred yards and you'll see the Pacific, and other points north of here.

Adult American Bald eagle

INTRODUCTION TO THE DIAMOND PEAK WILDERNESS

Wildflowers dance in the wind. Elk bugle during the fall rut. Deer tiptoe quietly through dense forests. Marmots chase each other over boulder fields, their antics like children at the local playground. Clear mountain streams crisscross the land. Deep blue lakes dot the landscape. Formed by angry volcanic activity, many of the lakes fill depressions, scratched out of the surface by mighty glaciers. And above it all stands the guardian of the Wilderness—Diamond Peak.

Located in the Cascade Mountains of central Oregon, the 8,744 foot peak is one of hundreds of old volcanoes that make up the expansive "Ring of Fire." At one time the mountain reached hundreds of feet higher into the heavens, but glaciers cut deeply into the immense mountain, gouging out glacial cirques and chopping Diamond Peak down to its present size.

On February 5, 1957 the Forest Service established the Diamond Peak Wild Area. Later, in 1964, it was reclassified wilderness by the Wilderness Act.

Upon establishment, 36,637 acres of wilderness gained protection. Later, with passage of the Oregon Wilderness Act of 1984, the Wilderness increased to its present size—52,329 acres.

Diamond Peak is the area's most prominent peak, with two other tall peaks, Mt. Yoran and Lakeview Mountain, reaching high into the heavens as well. Climbers bag summits on all three peaks. The most popular route to Diamond Peak's lofty summit is from the south ridge. Although not a difficult climb, one should never attempt to reach the summit alone.

Mt. Yoran, at 7,138 feet, offers skilled mountaineers the chance to scale a steep precipice. Experienced climbers scale Lakeview Mountain as well.

Both the Willamette and Deschutes National Forests manage the Wilderness. The Willamette cares for 19,762 acres of preserve, the Deschutes 32,567 acres. Both agencies maintain trails on a yearly basis.

Approximately 125 miles of trails penetrate the area which ranges in elevation from 4,787 feet near Odell Lake to a high of 8,744 feet atop Diamond Peak. The Pacific Crest National Scenic Trail (PCNST) divides the area, skirting the east slope of Diamond Peak from north to south.

While today's visitors come to hike, hunt, fish, photograph, and just relax, a century ago folks came for other reasons. For instance, the hardy members of the "Lost Wagon Train" came searching for the Willamette Valley. En route from Allegheny City, Pennsylvania, during October of 1853, the pioneers hoped to find a primitive road leading over the mountains to the fertile valley. They found none, however.

With winter just around the corner, the wagon train members were desperate to reach the other side of the mountain. On they pushed, up through the mountains, carving a rough road in the harsh landscape. Hardy folks that they were, they inched forward, probably guided by the snow-covered slopes of Diamond Peak. (John Diamond scaled the peak the previous year in an attempt to look for a pass through the mountains. The peak was named for him.)

West of the summit, the pioneers were nearly heartbroken as they viewed a sea of timber stretching out before them. Too close to give up, they sent out one of their men for help. A rescue party from the valley met the 1,500 starving pioneers and everyone reached safety and the town of Butte Disappointment (known as Lowell today).

Although distraught at the time, the pioneers undoubtedly realized that the area was rich in timber and other vegetation. Douglas fir and western hemlock blanket most of Diamond Peak's west side. True fir, mountain hemlock and western white pine cover much of the remaining area. Also, there are dense stands of lodgepole pines in the eastern half of the Wilderness. Thick understory carpets much of the ground in the true fir-hemlock forest. Huckleberries and dwarf manzanita are the most common.

There are many species of wildflowers to see, smell, touch, and enjoy. Look for lupine, trillium, penstemon, Indian paint brush, shooting stars, rhododendrons, and many more.

Wildlife is abundant as well, but rarely seen. Mammals are especially difficult to spot. Black-tailed deer and elk spend much of the year in the Wilderness. When winter descends upon the area, the mule deer migrate eastward. Heading out of the preserve, they travel down to the sage desert. Black-tailed deer and elk descend the west slope. Bear and small mammals, such as marmots, snowshoe rabbits, pine martens, foxes, squirrels, and pika inhabit the area all year long.

There are many species of bird life. Most common include the dipper or water ouzel and the grouse. Other species observed are the Clark's nutcracker, gray jay, Oregon junco, and raven. Bufflehead,goldeneye, and wood ducks nest near some of the lakes.

Mosquitoes are the most abundant critter of this high mountain area during June and July. However, August through October are relatively mosquito-free.

As in all mountainous regions, the weather changes very quickly. Wear proper clothing (several layers are better than one) and remember that nights are cool regardless of daytime temperatures. Snow blankets portions of the high trails well into July in some years. Be prepared for snow travel.

During the winter, Diamond Peak is popular with cross-country skiers and people sporting the latest in snowshoes. Hardy souls climb Diamond Peak during the cold, long months of winter.

The Forest Service requires wilderness permits from June 15 through November 15. All visitors should sign-up at a nearby District Ranger Office. The permits are free of charge and provide valuable information toward future management of the area by the Forest Service.

For more information contact:

Deschutes National Forest
Crescent Ranger District
P.O. Box 208
Crescent, OR. 97733
(503) 433-2234

or

Willamette National Forest
Rigdon Ranger District
48455 Highway 58
Oakridge, OR. 97463
(503) 782-2283

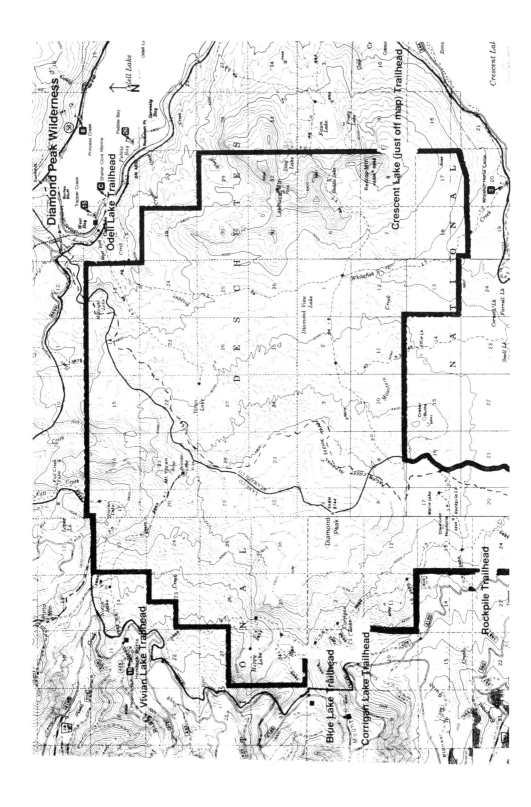

CENTRAL OREGON WILDERNESS AREAS

2 VIVIAN LAKE TRAILHEAD TO DIVIDE LAKE

Distance: 4.0 miles (one-way)
Elevation gain: 1,280 feet; loss 160 feet
High point: 6,400 feet
Usually open: July through October
Topographic map: Diamond Peak
                  Wilderness Map
Obtain map from: Deschutes National
                  Forest or Willamette
                  National Forest

The trail leading to Divide Lake offers good views of Diamond Peak and numerous Cascade Peaks. Snug in the northwest corner of the Diamond Peak Wilderness, the trail leads through dense old-growth forest before reaching Divide Lake. From the lake, a spectacular view of 7,138 foot Mount Yoran is possible.

To reach the trailhead near Hemlock Butte, travel to the small town of Crescent Lake, located on Oregon Highway 58, 35 miles southeast of Oakridge. At Crescent Lake you'll find a cafe, gas, food, and supplies.

Head southwest on paved Crescent Lake Road and reach a junction of FS Road No. 60 at 2.3 miles. (Wilderness map states this is Road No. 244.) Turn right at the sign: "Summit Lake - 12 miles." Follow the paved road along the north end of Crescent Lake to the junction of FS Road No. 6010, another 5.1 miles down the road. (Map claims this is Road No. 211.)

Turn right onto Road No. 6010, traveling the unmaintained dirt road (passenger cars okay) to Emigrant Pass, another 6.6 miles away. Summit Lake and campground are to your left as you head right on FS Road No. 380. Soon after, pass the Pacific Crest Trailhead.

Continue for another mile or so, then the road turns to a good gravel road. At 2.3 miles from Emigrant Pass turn right on FS Road No. 2160. Drive 4.1 miles on this road until you reach FS Road No. 2149 and a sign "Bear Mountain." Head to the right and continue traveling Road No. 2149. Look for a beautiful little waterfall on the right, as you drive another 9.1 miles to the junction of FS Road No. 23 and a sign: "Vivian Lake - 4 miles."

Turn right on Road No. 23 (Map states Road No. 2145) and reach the trailhead near Hemlock Butte after 4.1 miles.

A terrific view of Diamond Peak greets you as you begin hiking Vivian Lake Trail No. 3662. Enter the Wilderness about 100 yards down the trail and reach the forest shortly thereafter.

From this point begin a gradual climb to Notch Lake and a couple other unnamed lakes at 0.7 mile. Notch Lake is good for fishing with trout caught one after the other the day we visited the area. Anglers will most likely hook rainbow and brook trout in this scenic four-acre lake. Those spending the night will find several campsites around the lake.

At 0.9 mile reach the junction to Mount Yoran and Vivian Lake. Head to the right on Mount Yoran Trail No. 3683 climbing at a moderate rate, then switchback up a couple of times after the 2.2 miles mark.

Reach a saddle at 2.5 miles. To the north you'll see the Three Sisters, Broken Top, and Mount Washington. And on a clear day it's possible to see the outline of Oregon's highest peak, Mount Hood. Also as you hike, see Diamond Peak through the trees to the south.

Hike the saddle at a level or gradual decline then up to one-acre Divide Lake at 4.0 miles. We visited the area in early July, when snow covered portions of the trail. A thin layer of ice blanketed most of Divide Lake, with several small openings visible around the lakes outer edge. Snow covered portions of the campsites, but there appeared to be a couple of flat sites on the south and west sides of the lake.

Those interested in fishing take note: some Forest Service employees claim the "fishing is very poor at Divide Lake." However, a Forest Service hiking supplement brags, "Divide Lake contains cutthroat trout and provides the angler a little-used wilderness fishing opportunity." Try it for yourself and see!

Divide Lake and Mt. Yoran

CENTRAL OREGON WILDERNESS AREAS

3 VIVIAN LAKE TRAILHEAD TO VIVIAN LAKE

Distance: 3.8 miles (one-way)
Elevation gain: 720 feet; loss 560 feet
High point: 6,000 feet
Usually open: July through October
Topographic map: Diamond Peak
                 Wilderness Map
Obtain map from: Deschutes National
                 Forest or Willamette
                 National Forest

Hikers traveling this popular trail go through dense forest and pass by several small lakes. In the early summer months flowers border Fall Creek.

To reach the trailhead near Hemlock Butte, travel 35 miles southeast of Oakridge via Oregon Highway 58 to the small town of Crescent Lake. At Crescent Lake you'll find a cafe, gas, food, and supplies.

Head southwest on paved Crescent Lake Road and reach a junction of FS Road No. 60 at 2.3 miles. (Wilderness Map states this is Road No. 244.) Turn right at the sign: "Summit Lake - 12 miles." Drive the paved road along the north end of Crescent Lake to the junction of FS Road No. 6010, another 5.1 miles down the road. (Map claims this is Road No. 211.)

Turn right onto Road No. 6010, traveling the unmaintained dirt road (passenger cars okay) to Emigrant Pass, another 6.6 miles away. Summit Lake and campground are to your left as you head right on FS Road No. 380. Soon after, pass the Pacific Crest Trailhead.

Continue for another mile or so then the road turns to a good gravel road. At 2.3 miles from Emigrant Pass turn right on FS Road No. 2160. Drive 4.1 miles on this road until you reach FS Road No. 2149 and a sign "Bear Mountain." Head to the right and continue traveling Road No. 2149. Notice the waterfall on the right, as you drive another 9.1 miles to the junction of FS Road No. 23 and a sign: "Vivian Lake - 4 miles." Turn right on Road No. 23 (Map states Road No. 2145) and reach the trailhead near Hemlock Butte after 4.1 miles.

A fantastic view of Diamond Peak welcomes you as you begin hiking Vivian Lake Trail No. 3662. Reach the Wilderness boundary about 100 yards down the trail and enter the forest shortly thereafter.

From this point begin a gradual climb to Notch Lake at 0.7 mile. Notch Lake is good fishing for brook and rainbow trout.

At 0.9 mile reach the junction to Mount Yoran and Vivian Lake. Head to the left, staying on Vivian Lake Trail, and hiking through the trees then up a short, steep pitch at 1.3 miles. At this point you'll come to the junction of Pinto Mountain Trail No. 3684. This trail leads to FS Road No. 510.

Continue straight, climbing at a gradual, sometimes moderate rate, to 2.1 miles. Now begin a steep descent then level off some and reach a small lake on your right at 2.6 miles. At 2.7 miles reach a larger unnamed lake with Mt. Yoran visible in the background and flat campsites nearby.

At 2.8 miles pass a lake to the left then begin a steep descent to cascading Fall Creek at 3.0 miles. Continue, hiking level now to 3.7 miles and the junction to Vivian Lake. Turn left, hiking across the meadow or around the first small lake to Vivian Lake at 3.8 miles. You'll find camp sites at various points around the lake.

Those interested in wildflowers will find many fine species around the lake in June and July. Anglers will find the fishing fine for brook trout in the 24-acre lake. At 15 feet deep, Vivian Lake is also nice for swimming.

4 FS ROAD NO. 2149 TO BLUE AND HAPPY LAKES

Distance: 3.2 miles (one-way)
Elevation gain: 400 feet; loss 640 feet
High point: 5,920 feet
Usually open: July through October
Topographic map: Diamond Peak
              Wilderness Map
Obtain map from: Deschutes National
              Forest or Willamette
              National Forest

Good fishing, hordes of frogs, scenic lakes, and colorful wildflowers—including rhododendrons—make this trip a special treat.

To reach the trailhead travel 35 miles southeast of Oakridge via Oregon Highway 58 to the small town of Crescent Lake. At Crescent Lake you'll find a cafe, gas, food, and supplies.

Head southwest on paved Crescent Lake Road and reach a junction of FS Road No. 60 at 2.3 miles. (Wilderness map states this is Road No. 244.) Turn right at the sign: "Summit Lake - 12 miles." Drive the paved road along the north end of Crescent Lake to the junction of FS Road No. 6010, another 5.1 miles down the road. (Map shows this as Road No. 211.)

Turn right onto Road No. 6010, traveling the unmaintained dirt road (passenger cars okay) to Emigrant Pass, another 6.6 miles away. Summit Lake and campground are to your left as you head right on FS Road No. 380. Soon after, pass the Pacific Crest Trailhead.

Continue traveling the dirt road for another mile or so then the road turns to a good gravel road. At 2.3 miles from Emigrant Pass turn right on FS Road No. 2160. Drive 4.1 miles on this road until you reach FS Road No. 2149 and a sign "Bear Mountain." Head to the right and continue 4.9 miles to the trailhead.

It's an easy hike to Blue Lake through the trees via Blue Lake Trail No. 3645 to the Wilderness boundary at 0.6 mile. (Look for western trillium and other flower species along the way.) The right fork leads 0.1 mile to a large camp at the south end of Blue Lake, one of the largest lakes in the Wilderness. Brook trout inhabit the 40 foot deep, 10-acre lake.

To continue to Happy Lake, head to the left, crossing over a creek at 0.7 mile. Go to the north end of the lake where you'll find a camp at 0.9 mile. The camp is too close to the lake. It's a good place, however, to look for frogs.

The trail turns abruptly at the camp, leading up the ridge via switchback. Although unsigned, the trail is easy to follow if you look for a blazed tree and a cut log. Hike at a moderate rate; then the grade lessens before reaching Diamond Peak Trail No. 3699 at 1.7 miles.

Head to the left, descending at a moderate, sometimes steep rate, and crossing two streams within a quarter mile of the junction. At 2.7 miles reach the junction to Happy Lake. Turn left on Happy Lake Trail No. 3653 and descend moderately to a wood bridge at 3.2 miles. Happy Lake is now visible to your left.

Rhododendrons line portions of the lake in July, creating a perfect photo opportunity. And in the extensive boggy meadows nearby, there are countless other species to enjoy. Mountain hemlock and western white pine surround the seven-acre lake, with Alaska huckleberry sprinkled over much of the forest floor.

Anglers may catch brook or rainbow trout at Vivian Lake. Those interested in frogs will find plenty of the slippery amphibians, especially in the boggy areas.

For added enjoyment, follow the stream to the north a short distance and hear the musical sound of water cascading down slippery rocks. Also, view Hemlock Butte and points beyond in the distance.

5 FS ROAD NO. 2149 TO CORRIGAN LAKE

Distance: 1.4 miles (one-way)
Elevation gain: 640 feet; loss 0 feet
High point: 5,600 feet
Usually open: July through October
Topographic map: Diamond Peak
Wilderness Map
Obtain map from: Deschutes National
Forest or Willamette
National Forest

Easy hikes are always a pleasure and the hike to Corrigan Lake is no exception. The reward, a terrific view of Diamond Peak, is tremendous for the little effort needed to reach Corrigan Lake. Hikers interested in photographing the lake should arrive in the afternoon.

To reach the trailhead drive 35 miles southeast of Oakridge via Oregon Highway 58 to the small town of Crescent Lake. At Crescent Lake you'll find a cafe, gas, food, and supplies.

Head southwest on paved Crescent Lake Road and reach a junction of FS Road No. 60 at 2.3 miles. (Wilderness map states this is Road No. 244.) Turn right at the sign: "Summit Lake - 12 miles." Drive the paved road along the north end of Crescent Lake to the junction of FS Road No. 6010, another 5.1 miles down the road. (Map shows this as Road No. 211.)

Turn right onto Road No. 6010, traveling the unmaintained dirt road (passenger cars okay) to Emigrant Pass, another 6.6 miles away. Summit Lake and campground are to your left as you head right on FS Road No. 380. Soon after, pass the Pacific Crest Trailhead.

Continue for another mile or so then the road turns to a good gravel road. At 2.3 miles from Emigrant Pass turn right on FS Road No. 2160. Drive 4.1 miles on this road until you reach FS Road No. 2149 and a sign "Bear Mountain." Head to the right and continue to the trailhead at 1.2 miles.

Corrigan Lake Trail No. 3654 leads through the trees, roaming amidst a lush alpine forest of mountain hemlock and grand, silver, and noble fir. Hike at a gradual rate and cross the Wilderness boundary in 100 yards.

Switchback up at 0.3 mile and again at 0.7 mile; then wind up the slope and reach a junction at 1.4 miles. Diamond Peak Trail is straight ahead. Head to the right and towards Corrigan Lake, 100 yards away.

Diamond Peak provides a splendid backdrop for Corrigan Lake when viewed from the west. Fishermen will find the fishing equally splendid, with brook trout hooked often. Those spending the night will find an informal trail bordering the five-acre lake, with several campsites located off the trail.

Alpine Shooting Star

Marie Lake

CENTRAL OREGON WILDERNESS AREAS

6 DIAMOND ROCKPILE TRAILHEAD TO MARIE LAKE

Distance: 2.4 miles
Elevation gain: 960 feet; loss 160 feet
High point: 6,160 feet
Usually open: July through October
Topographic map: Diamond Peak
Wilderness Map
Obtain map from: Deschutes National
Forest or Willamette
National Forest

The trail to Marie Lake offers good views of Mount Thielsen, Sawtooth Mountain and Cowhorn Mountain, all which provide a magnificent backdrop to Summit Lake. At Marie Lake, there's the chance to swim in crystal clear waters, and the opportunity to catch brook trout.

To reach the trailhead at Diamond Rockpile Trailhead, travel to Crescent Lake. The tiny town sits on Oregon Highway 58, 35 miles southeast of Oakridge. At Crescent Lake you'll find a cafe, gas, food, and supplies.

Head southwest on paved Crescent Lake Road and reach a junction of FS Road No. 60 at 2.3 miles. (Wilderness map states this is Road No. 244.) Turn right at the sign: "Summit Lake - 12 miles." Follow the paved road along the north end of Crescent Lake to the junction of FS Road No. 6010, another 5.1 miles down the road. (Map shows this as Road No. 211.)

Turn right onto Road No. 6010, traveling the unmaintained dirt road (passenger cars okay) to Emigrant Pass, another 6.6 miles away. Summit Lake and campground are to your left as you head right on FS Road No. 380. Soon after, pass the Pacific Crest Trailhead.

Continue driving the dirt road for another mile or so, then the road turns to a good gravel road. At 2.3 miles from Emigrant Pass, turn right on FS Road No. 2160. Travel 1.6 miles farther to the Diamond Rockpile Trailhead. You'll find plenty of room to park here.

Begin hiking Diamond Rockpile Trail No. 3632 (now called the Rockpile Trail) traveling through a previously logged area where little pines now grow. Hike on a moderate grade, entering the Wilderness at 0.4 mile.

Now hike through the trees, continuing at a moderate, occasionally steep grade. At 0.9 mile reach the junction of the Diamond Peak Trail. Stay straight.

Gradually climb to 1.6 miles and a good view of Mount Thielsen and Sawtooth Mountain through the trees. Level off some at 1.7 miles and cross a semi-open slope at 1.8 miles. To the south there is a magnificent view of Summit Lake, with Cowhorn and Sawtooth Peaks and Mount Thielsen visible, from left to right.

Descend gradually to 2.2 miles and a junction. To reach the Pacific Crest Trail (PCT), head to the right. Turn left, and follow the creek to Marie Lake at 2.4 miles. There are a couple of campsites located at Marie Lake, one on the east side of the lake, one on the west side. Both are too close to the water.

Diamond Peak is not visible from the lake, but may be viewed by climbing the ridge to the northeast of the east side camp. It's about 100 feet to the top of the ridge where you'll find flat areas to camp.

Spreading out over 20 acres and reaching a depth of 35 feet, Marie Lake offers excellent fishing and swimming possibilities for young and old alike.

Diamond View Lake and Diamond Peak

CENTRAL OREGON WILDERNESS AREAS

7 DIAMOND VIEW LAKE/ DIAMOND PEAK LOOP

Distance: 23.3 miles
Elevation gain: 2,900 feet; loss 2,900 feet
High point: 7,040 feet
Usually open: July through October
Topographic map: Diamond Peak
    Wilderness Map
Obtain map from: Deschutes National
    Forest or Willamette
    National Forest

This loop has it all. From the high, east slopes of Diamond Peak, wide vistas abound. From the lower reaches of the Wilderness, hikers pass through a forest of skinny lodgepole pines, western white pine, mountain hemlock, and true firs. In addition, the loop passes by several scenic lakes, some with fantastic views of the core of the Diamond Peak Wilderness.

To reach the beginning of the loop at Odell Lake, drive to the West Odell Campground. The campground sits 28 miles southeast of Oakridge, via Oregon Highway 58. Turn right at the signed junction and descend FS Road No. 5810 (Odell Lake Rd.), reaching the trailhead for Mount Yoran Lake at 1.8 miles.

Begin hiking Mount Yoran Trail No. 49 by crossing the railroad tracks, then climbing gradually through the trees to a junction at 0.2 mile. To the right lies the Willamette Pass. Mount Yoran lies straight ahead. To begin the loop, head left on Whitefish Trail No. 42 to Crescent Lake - 11 miles away.

From the junction it's a level walk to Trapper Creek and a bridge crossing at 0.4 mile. Follow the trail, which leads along the creek, then climb a short, steep pitch to an old trail leading from the West Odell Campground to this point.

Turn right, following Trapper Creek as it delights each observer with gallons of water cascading over rocks and boulders. Lush grasses and dwarf huckleberries blanket much of the forest floor; Englemann spruce and white fir stand tall.

Continue to a split in Trapper Creek at 1.2 miles. At this point, gradually move away from the creek and begin hiking through a stand of toothpick-thin lodgepole pines. At 3.0 miles there's a good view of Diamond Peak through the trees. Continue past two small ponds at 4.7 miles and reach Diamond View Lake at 5.0 miles.

As you may have guessed, there is a terrific view of the 8,744 foot extinct volcano from this lake. Several camps rest around the lake, with many of the east shore sites located less than 100 feet from the shoreline. Please don't camp here.

The fishing is lousy at Diamond View Lake. The Oregon Department of Fish and Wildlife does not stock the lake. As far as they know, fish do not exist in the lake. However, it more than makes up for its poor fishing with a wonderful view.

At 5.2 miles reach the south end of Diamond View Lake, and continue south to a small lake at 5.4 miles. Pass several more ponds before arriving at a junction at 5.8 miles. Head right on Crater Butte Trail No. 44 which leads to the Pacific Crest Trail (PCT).

Gradually climb through the trees, following along a creek after 6.6 miles. At 7.7 miles reach the junction to Snell Lake. Keep straight. Reach heart-shaped Mountain View Lake at 8.4 miles, an area with plenty of flat sites for camping, and a gorgeous view of Diamond Peak. This is also a good spot to look for hardy climbers attempting to scale the summit of this high mountain peak.

Cross a stream at 8.7 miles, continuing through the trees at a gradual rate and cross another stream at 8.8 miles, following blazed trees when the trail isn't visible.

At 9.3 miles begin descending, hiking a gradual to moderate grade, curving to the right upon reaching a sign at 10.3 miles. Hike an old road now, and reach the junction of the Pacific Crest National Scenic Trail (PCNST) at 10.5 miles. Turn right to continue the loop up the PCT.

Those needing a nice spot to camp should note that camp sites are available at nearby Marie and Rockpile Lakes. To reach these lakes stay straight, descending gradually via Rockpile Trail No. 3632, an old road, to the turnoff for Rockpile Lake 0.4 mile from the PCT. Turn left and reach the lake in 0.1 mile. There are plenty of campsites at the south end of the lake. Also, there's an old trapper's cabin to explore. Anglers will find brook trout in the six-acre lake.

To reach Marie Lake, head another 0.5 mile north to 20-acre Marie Lake, a good fishing lake. Campsites are available on both the east and west end of the lake, but both sites are within 100 feet of the shoreline.

Back on the PCT, hike north traveling through the trees and up at a gradual grade to 10.9 miles and a stream. From there wind up the slope to 11.7 miles and a fantastic view of Summit Lake to the south. Cowhorn Mountain, Sawtooth Mountain, Mt. Thielsen, Mt. Bailey, and numerous other Cascade peaks, provide a splendid backdrop to the deep blue lake.

This point also marks a popular exit point for those hiking up the South Spur en route to the summit of Diamond Peak. Red flags mark the beginning of the route, then it's a steep climb to the open ridge.

Head back into the trees, then out in the open for a good look at Diamond Peak at 12.7 miles. Also, see Crescent Lake to the east. Terrific views are common along this portion of the PCT as you hike along the east slope of Diamond Peak. Stunted mountain hemlock stand scattered throughout the area where rivers of giant boulders once flowed.

Cross several small streams (most flow year-round), hiking both below and above timberline. Reach an open area and good view of the Three Sisters and surrounding peaks at 14.5 miles. At 14.7 miles see Odell Lake off to the right and the scarred Willamette Pass Ski area is clearly visible as well. Continue to 15.4 miles and a good view of Mount Yoran to the north. Cross a couple more streams, then reach a small lake at 16.3 miles. From here there are spectacular views of Diamond Peak, Mount Yoran, Three Sisters, Fuji Mountain, and Odell Lake. Also, on a clear day see Mount Washington, Mount Jefferson, Three-Fingered Jack, and Mount Hood to the north.

Descend now, heading down into the trees. After a short distance, pass several small pools before heading to another pool directly below the south peak of Mount Yoran at 17.2 miles.

During the next few miles there are several good views of Diamond Peak. The trail passes by numerous lakes and ponds before reaching a spur trail leading to Midnight Lake at 21.3 miles. Continue to a junction at 21.5 miles where a blue sign points the way back to Midnight Lake or straight ahead to the Gold Lake Snow Park, 2.7 miles away.

Head straight from this point and reach the Wilderness boundary at 22.5 miles. Turn left on an old road and go 200 feet to another blue signed junction. Turn right to reach Odell Lake Road. Cross railroad tracks at 23.0 miles and continue 100 yards to paved Odell Lake Road. Turn right, completing the loop at 23.3 miles.

Stag Lake and Lakeview Mountain

CENTRAL OREGON WILDERNESS AREAS

8 CRESCENT LAKE TRAIL-HEAD TO STAG LAKE

Distance: 4.7 miles
Elevation gain: 1,100 feet; loss 45 feet
High point: 5,840 feet
Usually open: July through October
Topographic map: Diamond Peak
                             Wilderness Map
Obtain map from: Deschutes National
                             Forest or Willamette
                             National Forest

The trail to Stag Lake begins at popular Crescent Lake, a mecca for campers and water enthusiasts. On summer weekends the trail is often crowded. If you're yearning for solitude, try hiking the trail on a weekday.

The trail is perfect for family day hikes, especially for couples with small children, as it is a gradual grade up to Fawn and Stag Lakes.

To reach the trailhead drive to Crescent Lake, Oregon. The small town (with supplies) rests 35 miles southeast of Oakridge on Oregon Hwy. 58. Head southwest on paved Crescent Lake Road for 2.3 miles to the junction of FS Road No. 60. (Wilderness map states this is FS Rd. No. 244.) Turn right and then left after driving another 0.4 mile to the Crescent Lake campground turnoff. Drive 0.2 mile down the dirt road to a large parking area. Turn right and head to the north end of the parking area to the trailhead sign.

Fawn Lake Trail No. 44-A begins at the sign. Hike to the north, then cross FS Road No. 60 in one hundred yards and reenter a fairly open stand of lodgepole pine. Reach the wilderness boundary at 0.2 mile.

Hike at a gradual grade and come to an old road at 1.0 mile. Soon after the landscape changes as you enter a dense forest of giant Douglas fir and mountain hemlock. True firs also exist here. Later, pass through a forest of primarily lodgepole and western white pines.

Reach Fawn Lake at 3.2 miles. Lakeview Mountain provides a nice background for Fawn Lake with Redtop Mountain providing an equally vivid background a bit farther down the trail. There are potential camp-sites located around the lake. The first one you'll reach—complete with log picnic table and bench—is too close to the water. Please do not camp here.

Stretching out across 43 acres, Fawn Lake is a good fishing lake with populations of brook and rainbow trout. The lake is 27 feet deep and also good for swimming.

To continue to Stag Lake, follow the trail around the north end of the lake to a junction at 3.3 miles. This is the end of the Fawn Lake Trail and the beginning of Crater Butte Trail No. 44. Crater Butte Trail heads north to Odell Lake or west to the Pacific Crest Trail (PCT). Head straight, traveling toward the PCT.

Reach the old Wilderness boundary about 100 yards before the junction to Stag Lake at 4.2 miles. Turn right on Stag Lake Trail No. 44-B, traveling a nearly level grade through a forest of mountain hemlock and lodgepole pine to a small lake at 4.6 miles. Continue past this lake and reach Stag Lake another 0.1 mile away.

There's a great view of Lakeview Mountain from Stag Lake. On a windless day it's especially nice for the high craggy peak is reflected in the clear waters of the 27 foot deep lake.

Anglers will find brook and rainbow trout in this scenic lake. Several campsites make life easy for the overnighter.

INTRODUCTION TO THE DRIFT CREEK WILDERNESS

The Drift Creek Wilderness is a land of plenty. There are steep-sided canyons, abundant wildlife, and a tremendous stand of old-growth rain forest. Horseback riding is prohibited due to the fragile soil. It is a hiker's mecca.

At one time this was a mecca for the Alsea Indians as well. The Waldport-based Indians hunted here regularly and also gathered berries and other edibles. Later (prior to World War II), the white man appeared and tried, but did not successfully homestead the meadow you'll pass through while hiking the Drift Creek Wilderness.

Designated wilderness in 1984 with the signing of the Oregon Wilderness Act, few trails penetrate the 5,767 acre preserve. The Siuslaw National Forest manages eight miles, most of which receives semi-annual maintenance. Ranging in elevation from a low of 120 feet along Drift Creek to 1605 feet atop a nameless peak, the preserve lies 12 miles east of Waldport and 57 miles west of Corvallis.

Mild temperatures prevail year-round. Snow is rare, but rain is not. Heavy rainfall normally occurs from fall through spring, with 120 inches pelting Table Mountain. A mere 74 inches falls to the west.

Sitka spruce, Douglas fir and western hemlock dominate the region. Growing seven feet thick in some places, many of the largest trees are found along the Horse Creek Trail. Bigleaf maple trees line the creeks. Moss, licorice ferns, sourgrass, oxalis and other plants blanket the forest floor. During the summer, look for scrumptious berries including salmonberry, thimbleberry, huckleberries (both the red and blue varieties), and salal. Roosevelt elk, black-tailed deer and black bear inhabit the forest surrounding Drift Creek. The northern spotted owl nests here and our nation's symbol, the American bald eagle, has been sighted on occasion.

Huge runs of Chinook salmon, coho salmon, steelhead and cutthroat trout are found in Drift Creek, a tributary of the Alsea River. The fishing is excellent and is managed for native fish only. This region is also a moderately popular hunting area during the proper season.

For more information contact:

Forest Supervisor
Waldport Ranger District
P.O. Box 400
Waldport, OR 97394
(503) 563-3211

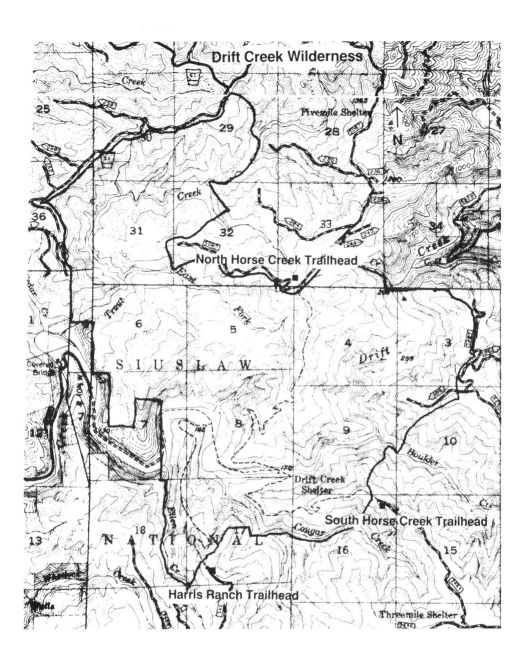

9 NORTH HORSE CREEK TRAIL

Distance: 3.2 miles (one-way)
Elevation gain: 1380 feet; loss 50 feet
High point: 1500 feet
Usually open: Year round
Topographic map: U.S.G.S. Tidewater,
Oregon 1956
Obtain map from: U.S.G.S.—Denver, CO.

Horse Creek Trail is really one trail, but I have divided it in two calling them the North and South Horse Creek Trails. Because the two trailheads are quite a few miles apart, most people will probably want to hike up the same trail they hike down.

The northern portion of Horse Creek Trail traverses spectacular old-growth forest and lush vegetation. On your way down to the creek look for banana slugs, newts, and in the creek itself, crayfish.

To reach the North Horse Creek Trailhead, travel 0.8 mile north of Yachats, a small coastal town with all the amenities. From U.S. Hwy. 101, head east on Bayview Road (County Road No. 701). A sign reading "Drift Creek" points the way.

The paved road leads 4.2 miles before turning to a good gravel road. In another 1.0 mile come to North Bayview Road: stay to the left. Travel an additional 1.0 mile to a fork. Head left on paved FS Road No. 51. Drive 4.0 miles staying right on FS Road No. 51 as the road becomes gravel again.

Come to a fork in 1.8 miles. Head right again, driving towards North Beaver Creek and Toledo. At 1.1 miles Road No. 51 curves to the left. Stay straight, now driving paved FS Road No. 50. Drive another 1.4 miles and turn right on gravel FS Road No. 5087. A sign, "Horse Creek Trail" points the way. Reach the trailhead in 3.5 miles.

Begin hiking the easy trail, entering the Wilderness in 100 feet. The trail is a gradual up and down (mostly down) for the first 1.4 miles. As you hike, gaze at the spectacular forest around you: massive Douglas fir, western hemlock and red cedar reach for the heavens. Notice the moss clinging to the trees and a variety of plants. See numerous species of ferns swaying in the breeze. Look for spotted owls and other wildlife, and in the spring, enjoy the wildflowers that dot the surrounding landscape.

About midway through the hike the trail steepens, moderately descending to Drift Creek at 3.2 miles. Just prior to reaching the creek, you'll come to a fork. Head to the left for 50 yards for a good view of the creek and a nice place for a picnic. If you'd like to continue up South Horse Creek Trail, you'll have to ford the creek (see #10, South Horse Creek Trail for more information). The Forest Service claims Drift Creek can be forded during most summer months.

To continue along the creek, head to the right via the Harris Ranch Trail. (See #11, Harris Ranch Trail for more information.) The trail continues at a mostly level grade, through dense vegetation, reaching the creek and a necessary ford another 0.8 mile away.

Camp sites are limited in the Drift Creek Wilderness. Although someone has camped near the creek on the Horse Creek Trail, it is really too close to the water. In addition, it's rocky, isn't level and there isn't room for a tent. The best campsites are located near the meadow and creek on the Harris Ranch Trail.

(Upon reaching Drift Creek, you may be wondering "Where is Horse Creek?" Horse Creek actually flows near Toledo. Originally, however, the trail stretched from Tidewater to Horse Creek.)

10 SOUTH HORSE CREEK TRAIL

Distance: 2.3 miles (one-way)
Elevation gain: 1310 feet; loss 0 feet
High point: 1480 feet
Usually open: Year round
Topographic map: U.S.G.S. Tidewater,
　　　　　　　　Oregon 1956
Obtain map from: U.S.G.S.—Denver, CO.

Horse Creek Trail is really one trail, but I have divided it in two as most hikers will probably want to hike up the same trail they hike down. The two trailheads, North and South Horse Creek, are quite a few miles apart, making a car shuttle impractical. For convenience sake I've called the trails the North and South Horse Creek Trails.

South Horse Creek Trail leads to Drift Creek and an assortment of fun for it's a beautiful place to picnic, fish or relax. Those with a shuttle available could begin hiking at the Harris Ranch Trailhead—a steeper descent— (see #11, Harris Ranch Trail for more information) and hike back via this trail.

If you'd like to spend the night, there's a good spot to camp near the old Harris Ranch homestead. To make this trip possible, you'd have to ford Drift Creek twice. The Forest Service recommends crossing the creek in the summer months only. A ford is possible during *most* summer months.

Reach the South Horse Creek Trailhead by driving 7.1 miles east of Waldport via County Road 34. From U.S. Hwy. 101 in this coastal town, a sign points the way to "Alsea." Necessary supplies are obtainable in Waldport, if necessary.

Cross the Alsea River after driving the 7.1 miles mentioned previously, and turn left on E. Risley Creek Road. You'll reach a fork shortly after turning; head to the right on FS Road No. 3446. At 2.6 miles the paved road turns to good gravel. Travel another 0.4 mile and reach a fork. Head to the right.

Drive 1.2 miles and head left if you're starting at the Harris Ranch Trailhead. If you'd rather begin at the South Horse Creek Trailhead or need to drop off a shuttle car, drive 4.5 miles to FS Road No. 3464 and a sign reading, "South Horse Creek Trailhead."

Turn left, reaching the trailhead in 1.6 miles.

Begin hiking through dense old-growth forest of Douglas fir and western hemlock. Look for red cedar and Sitka spruce as you travel through moist areas. An array of plant life covers the forest floor. There are red huckleberry, vine maple, sword fern, salal, trillium, coral root and foxglove to name a few.

Descend at a moderate grade to Drift Creek at 2.3 miles. There is no place to camp, but there are rock slabs for a dry picnic and the chance to do some fishing. The chance of catching a savory trout is high. Drift Creek contains wild runs of Chinook and coho salmon, as well as steelhead and cutthroat trout.

Ford the creek to continue to both the Harris Ranch and North Horse Creek Trails.

On a special note, as you hike along these trails, don't bother looking for Horse Creek. It's located near Toledo. In case you were wondering, at one time Horse Creek Trail stretched from Tidewater to Horse Creek.

Drift Creek

CENTRAL OREGON WILDERNESS AREAS

11 HARRIS RANCH TRAIL

Distance: 3.2 miles (one-way)
Elevation gain: 1108 feet; loss 20 feet
High point: 1250 feet
Usually open: Year round
Topographic map: U.S.G.S. Tidewater,
                 Oregon 1956
Obtain map from: U.S.G.S.—Denver, CO.

Harris Ranch is the steepest of the three trails leading to Drift Creek, but it's worth the effort if you'd like a nice campsite along Drift Creek or if you enjoy exploring meadows.

Reach the Harris Ranch Trailhead by driving 7.1 miles east of Waldport via County Road 34. From U.S. Hwy. 101 in this coastal town, a sign points the way to "Alsea." Waldport has all kinds of supplies including food, gas and lodging.

Cross the Alsea River and turn left off of Road 34, now traveling E. Risley Creek Road. You'll reach a fork shortly after turning; head to the right on FS Road No. 3446. At 2.6 miles the paved road turns to good gravel. Travel another 0.4 mile and reach a fork. Head to the right.

Drive 1.2 miles and turn left on FS Road No. 346. A sign reads "Harris Ranch Trailhead." Reach a fork in 0.7 mile and stay to the left, reaching the trailhead another 0.2 mile down the road.

It's a short gradual climb up a small hill, then a moderate descent through lush old-growth forest of Douglas fir, western hemlock and cedar. The forest floor is carpeted with red huckleberry, vine maple, salmonberry, salal, foxglove, trillium, and oxalis. At 1.2 miles the trail levels off somewhat but the break lasts for less than one-half mile. Now you'll drop at a moderate to steep grade, reaching Drift Creek Meadow at 2.2 miles.

Before the meadow look to the right and see an old fireplace, now covered with moss, banana slugs and a variety of plants, including daffodils. This and a few stove parts is all that remains of the old Harris Ranch homestead.

According to Forest Service records, Fred Purath, a bachelor, operated a subsistence type farm in this location, and ran a few head of cattle. Fred was a loner, walking into town perhaps once a year. In the early 1940s, Earl Harris purchased the land.

After entering the meadow you'll see two trails, one a faint trail heading to the south. The Harris Ranch Trail leads south 0.2 mile across the meadow, back into the trees, and bumps into Drift Creek. Ford the creek and continue at a mostly level grade along the creek 0.8 mile farther to both the North and South Horse Creek Trails. (See #9, North Horse Creek Trail and #10, South Horse Creek Trail for more information. Those with two cars may want to park one at the South Horse Creek Trailhead, hike down the steeper Harris Ranch Trail, and hike back via the easier trail.) Please note: the Forest Service recommends crossing Drift Creek during the summer months when the water level is low.

Back at the meadow, continue along the well-worn trail a hundred yards or so, heading back into the trees. You'll find some good campsites here. Most offer level ground, trees for shade and shelter, and a view of slab-lined Drift Creek.

Anglers will find excellent opportunities for hooking dinner. There are wild runs of Chinook and Coho salmon, as well as steelhead, and cutthroat trout. If you're not into fishing, look for deer and elk in the meadow.

INTRODUCTION TO THE MENAGERIE WILDERNESS

Lush forest stretches out across the steep, dissected, slopes of the Menagerie Wilderness. Lofty rock spires and arches—defiant lava intrusions—decorate the solitary landscape. It's a land like no other.

Heavy stands of 125-year-old Douglas fir, western hemlock and western red cedar blanket the area. Vine maple, salal, and sword fern cover most of the forest floor. Here and there, dozens of rock spires reach to the stars, drawing mountaineers from around the Pacific Northwest for technical climbing challenges.

Menagerie's spires are called a "menagerie" of animal names. These include Rabbit Ears, Turkey Monster (a 300-foot pinnacle, unclimbed until 1966), but perhaps the most famous is Rooster Rock. Others include Roosters Tail, Chicken Rock, Hen Rock, the Porpoise, and the Bridge. Two natural arches also grace the area.

Climbing difficulty ranges vary. A class 5.4 skill is required to reach Rooster Rock's abandoned lookout. Three other routes up to the same point range in difficulty to level II-5.8. Big Arch, one of two natural arches, is a level II-5.7-A1 climb. South Rabbit Ear, a 265-foot pinnacle, rates a III-5.7 climb, and North Rabbit Ear rates a III-5.7-A2. Turkey Monster has level III-5.6-A3 and level IV-5.7-A3 routes. The Porpoise rates a I-5.8 and the Bridge a II-5.9.

Climbers and hikers will find four miles of trails penetrating Oregon's smallest (excluding Oregon Islands) wilderness. Located 24 miles east of the town of Sweet Home, the 5,033-acre preserve ranges in elevation from 1,200 feet along State Highway 20 to 3,900 feet in the northern portion of the region. Managed by the Sweet Home Ranger District of the Willamette National Forest, the area rests on the western side of the Cascade Mountains.

The Forest Service reports that most of the area is used by day hikers, many of them rock climbers. Seventy-five percent reach the interior of the preserve via the Trout Creek/Rooster Rock trails. (See #13, Rooster Rock Trail and #12, Trout Creek Trail for more details.) Backpackers will find very little flat ground for camping.

Those choosing to backpack anyway, should note that all camps have to be located outside of view and at least 200 feet from any water sources, trails and other key interest features.

The Wilderness is open most of the year with year-round access possible from State Highway 20. Snow in the higher elevations usually prohibits access for two to three months during the winter.

Hikers, especially those who are quiet, have the chance to see deer, a questionable amount of elk, grouse and other species as well.

For more information contact:

Sweet Home Ranger District
3225 State Highway 20
Sweet Home, OR. 97386
(503)   367-5168

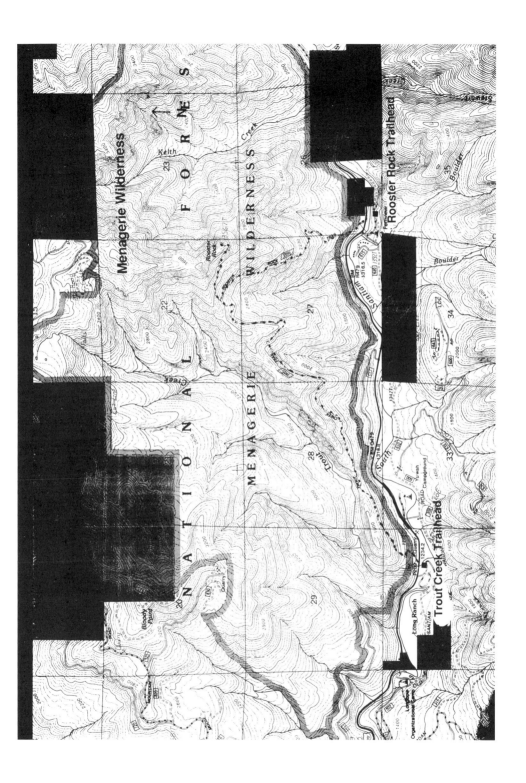

Climbers on Rooster Rock

CENTRAL OREGON WILDERNESS AREAS

12 TROUT CREEK TRAIL

Distance: 3.3 miles (one-way)
Elevation gain: 2,333 feet; loss 0 feet
High point: 3,567 feet
Usually open: Most of the year. Higher elevations snowed out for approximately 2 to 3 months.
Topographic map: U.S.G.S. Upper Soda, Oregon 1985
Obtain map from: U.S.G.S.—Denver, CO.

Trout Creek Trail begins near a popular campground of the same name—Trout Creek. Leading through dense forest comprised of second growth Douglas fir, the trail climbs to a high point near Rooster Rock, one of many spires located in the Wilderness.

To reach the trailhead, located 70 miles northeast of Eugene, travel on U.S. Highway 20 about 24 miles east of Sweet Home.

A marked trailhead is just past the entrance to the Trout Creek Campground, a lovely area with piped water. Facilities include pit toilets, picnic tables, BBQ pits, and a $5.00 fee during the summer months.

Begin hiking Trout Creek Trail No. 3405 traveling through dense vegetation, and entering the Wilderness in 100 yards. Stay on the well-defined trail when passing by several spur trails that are within 0.1 mile of the trailhead.

The trail leads up the slope at a gradual to moderate grade through a forest of Douglas fir. Some maple, alder, and madrone often mix in. A variety of plants cover the ground including ferns, manzanita, and rhododendrons.

At 2.4 miles you'll see Rooster Rock through the trees to the right. At 2.8 miles reach a trail junction. The trail to the right leads to the Fernview Campground. (See #13, Rooster Rock Trail for more information.)

Keep straight at the junction and reach Rooster Rock after a steep climb. Continue to a high point at 3.3 miles. From here there's a good view of the Wilderness and points in the distance.

A spring and pit toilet are located down the spur trail you'll see heading to the north.

It's about a 20 minute round-trip hike from the high point.

At one time there was a lookout atop the high, relatively flat point on which you are now standing. A watchman stood atop Rooster Rock with a cable ladder leading to the top of the spire. From this point there was a better view into the South Santiam River drainage.

Mule deer

13 ROOSTER ROCK TRAIL

Distance: 2.1 miles (one-way)
Elevation gain: 2,287 feet; loss 0 feet
High point: 3,567 feet
Usually open: Most of the year. Higher
elevations snowed out for
approximately 2 to 3
months.
Topographic map: U.S.G.S. Upper Soda,
Oregon 1985
Obtain map from: U.S.G.S.—Denver, CO.

Two trails lead to Rooster Rock. Trout Creek Trail (see #12, Trout Creek Trail) leads to the popular spire at an easy to moderate grade for most of the trip. The trail steepens, however, as it joins the Rooster Rock Trail for the last 0.5 mile trip to the top. Leading through a forest of second growth Douglas fir, Rooster Rock Trail climbs at a steep, but short grade to Rooster Rock.

To reach the trailhead, located 70 miles northeast of Eugene, travel east about 27 miles on U.S. Highway 20 from the town of Sweet Home.

You'll find the marked trailhead a short distance past the entrance to the Fernview Campground, a nice camp with all the necessities.

Begin hiking Rooster Rock No. 3399, traveling through dense vegetation, and entering the Wilderness in 100 yards. At 0.1 mile begin a steep grade that continues up through a forest of Douglas fir to 1.6 miles and the Trout Creek Trail junction.

Turn right and reach Rooster Rock after a steep climb. Continue to a high point at 2.1 miles. A terrific view of Rooster Rock, the Wilderness, and points beyond is available from this vantage point.

A spring and pit toilet are located down the spur trail you'll see heading off to the north. It's about a 20 minute round-trip hike from the high point.

At one time there was a lookout atop the high, relatively flat point on which you are now standing. And a watchman stood atop Rooster Rock with a cable ladder leading to the top of the spire. From this point there was a better view into the South Santiam River drainage.

Climber in the Menagerie Wilderness

CENTRAL OREGON WILDERNESS AREAS

INTRODUCTION TO THE MT. WASHINGTON WILDERNESS

It's always nice to find that special place, like the Mt. Washington Wilderness, where one can actually see nature at work. It seems as though we often forget about Mother Nature once the land is covered with trees, farm fields, cities and roads. We go about our daily business, rarely thinking of the role life's forces has entertained upon the earth on which we work, play and rest.

Upon reaching the Mt. Washington Wilderness, it is obvious that Mother Nature has indeed been hard at work. Hardened lava flows blanket much of the preserve, so much so that it is often called the "Black Wilderness."

If you like lava—enjoy its rugged sharp texture, like to imagine watching the flows of long ago—then you're in luck when venturing to this part of the Beaver State. You'll find 75 square miles of jagged lava flows to explore. The Pacific Crest National Scenic Trail (PCT) cuts through about four miles of the black stuff, passing an occasional bone-white snag as well. In addition, you'll see a hardy whitebark pine or two, small and stunted, like a Japanese bonsai tree. Hiking through the lava in the summer, you may see a hardy plant emerging from the ebony rock, colorful blossoms brightening up the dark surroundings.

But this 52,516 acre sanctuary is much more than lava. There are high mountain forests to hike and camp in, tall peaks—including the piercing point of Mt. Washington—to climb, and a myriad of clear blue lakes to swim and fish in.

Located 70 miles east of Eugene and 31 miles west of Bend, this High Cascade preserve stretches in elevation from a low of 3,000 feet near the western boundary to 7,794 feet atop its namesake, Mt.Washington. Spreading out across the Cascade Crest, the Wilderness is a mixed bag of tree species with mountain hemlock and true fir covering the plains and slopes surrounding the lava in the west; lodgepole and ponderosa pines blanketing the eastern slopes.

Managed by both the Deschutes and Willamette National Forests, this area was first protected as a Wild Area in 1957. In 1964, the Mt. Washington Wild Area became one of the first units of the newly created National Wilderness Preservation System. Thus, it became known as the Mt. Washington Wilderness.

Typical of numerous Cascade volcanoes, Mt. Washington developed during the Pleistocene Time (Ice Age) about two million years ago. Once a broad shield-shaped volcano, perhaps the size of nearby North Sister, glacier activity wore the huge mountain down to little more than the original plug. In other words, what you see today. It is a good example of a dissected volcano; only the lava filling remains.

Hikers will find plenty of recent volcanic activity in the surrounding area. In fact, this area is more active volcanically than other parts of the Oregon Cascades. User trails lead to the summits of both Mt. Washington and Belknap Crater, a cinder-and-ash cone with three distinct craters. A maintained trail leads to Little Belknap where you'll see excellent examples of volcanic spatter-cones, with conduits embracing both lava stalactites and stalagmites.

Since the Ice Age, no less than 125 different eruption centers manufactured cinder cones and basalt lava flows in this area. That's an average of one major eruption every century. The most recent flow, reaching twelve miles from Belknap Crater's flank to the McKenzie River, is 1300 years old.

Lava must have proven a problem for early travelers, but their determination proved tougher. An early Indian trail crosses south of the present-day McKenzie Pass. In 1860, the first route used by white men was opened by Felix Scott, Jr. and his party. They drove 900 cattle and nine wagons from the McKenzie River to Trout Creek in Jefferson County. Passing south of the present McKenzie Pass, the route was later called the Scott Trail.

In 1872, the McKenzie, Salt Springs and Deschutes Wagon Road Company completed a toll road over much of the present highway. The original road was covered with gravel in 1925 and paved in the early 1930's. Today, it's possible to see some of the original road, skirting the lava, near the Dee Wright Observatory.

Today's explorers include black-tailed deer and a few elk which inhabit the preserve in the summer when they follow the west slope up and over the crest. Mule deer, wintering in the Metolius Valley, climb the east slopes in the summertime. Black bear and an occasional cougar also live in the area. Small mammals include marmot, ground squirrel, pine marten, pika, coyote, fox and snowshoe rabbit.

Birds include ruffed and blue grouse, both game species. A variety of other bird species frequent the area in summer and may be seen by quiet and thoughtful observers.

Those interested in hunting or fishing (half of the area's 28 lakes are stocked with trout) should note that Oregon State Wildlife laws apply to all wild animals and fish found in the area. Check with the proper agency for more information.

Mountaineers travel up Mt. Washington's eroded lava plug all summer long. Technical climbs await those hungry for the top. These include a level I-4 North Ridge route, the first route climbed. A dozen more climbing routes increase in difficulty with a level III-5.7 on the east face and the level II-5.8 Chimney of Space on the west. Although some choose to climb without ropes or other equipment, the Forest Service suggests treating this as a technical climb. Rotten rock makes climbing without proper equipment even more dangerous.

Summers in the Mt. Washington Wilderness are usually warm and dry, winters are another story. Expect cold temperatures, wind and lots of snow. McKenzie Pass closes with the first big snow, sometime in November or December and opens again in May or June.

Trails are usually clear of snow and ready for hiking from mid-June to mid-October. Mosquitoes are atrocious early in the season; hikers seeking relief should wait until August to go into their favorite spots. In winter, nordic skiing is popular and provides a beautiful, bug-free recreational opportunity. Santiam Pass is open year-round and provides access into the Wilderness during this time of year.

For more information contact:

Willamette National Forest
McKenzie Ranger District
McKenzie Bridge, OR. 97413
(503) 822-3381

or

Deschutes National Forest
Sisters Ranger District
P.O. Box 249
Sisters, OR.   97759
(503)   549-2111

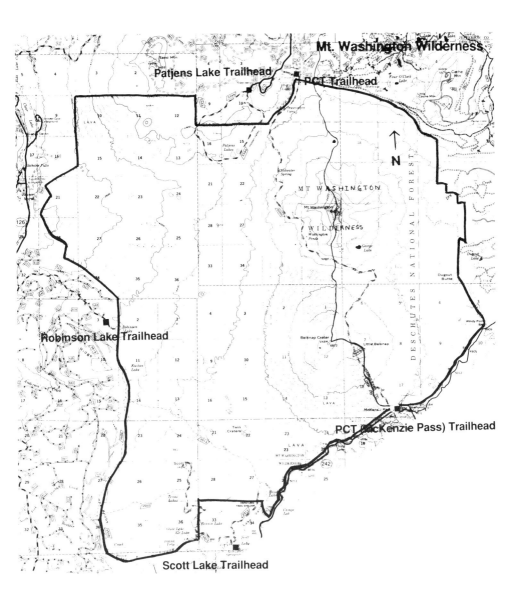

14 PATJENS LAKE LOOP

Distance: 5.8 miles (round-trip)
Elevation gain: 508 feet; loss 508 feet
High point: 4,800 feet
Usually open: July through October
Topographic map: The Mt. Washington Wilderness Map
Obtain map from: Deschutes National Forest, Willamette National Forest

Large crowds towing motorboats flock to Big Lake, starting point for the Patjens Lake Loop. But you can get away from the noisy motorboats with a peaceful jaunt to Patjens Lake. Along the way you'll view wildflowers (if you visit early in the season), and perhaps some illusive wildlife.

The trailhead is located 21 miles west of Sisters, off U.S. Hwy. 20. From the main highway, turn left (south) onto Big Lake Road (FS Road No. 2690) and reach the campground at Big Lake in 3.4 miles. If you'd like to set up a base camp at the lake, enter the improved campground and walk the road to the trailhead. If you're interested in a day hike or camping at Patjens Lakes, keep straight instead of entering the campground, reaching the trailhead in 0.6 mile.

There's plenty of room to park at the trailhead. Additional parking and campsites are located just south of it. There is no charge to camp here.

Hike through the trees to the south, reaching Patjens Lake Trail No. 3395 junction at 0.1 mile. Head either way to complete the loop. We went counterclockwise, walking to the right. The loop is easiest if hiked in this direction.

It's a gradual climb to 1.2 miles, then a gradual down to 1.3 miles and a trail leading right to the Cayuse Horse Camp. Continue through a forest comprised of lodgepole pine, western hemlock and alpine fir. Bear grass blankets the forest floor in July.

Encounter a steep grade after the last junction and the wilderness boundary sign at 1.6 miles. Reach a crest at 1.7 miles. Peer through the trees for a view of Mt. Washington and the Three Sisters. Begin descending the moderate to steep slope, watching for Cascade lilies, vanilla leaf and scarlet gilia. Also, you'll pass through an occasional fern-filled meadow.

There's an unnamed lake on the south side of the trail at 2.5 miles. A spur trail leads to water. Now it's a gradual up and down to 3.0 miles and the first of three Patjens Lakes. A side trail leads 0.1 mile around the west end of the lake to a camp and an excellent view of Mt. Washington. Ranging in size from three to six acres, the clear blue lakes are stocked with either brook or rainbow trout.

Back on the main trail, it's a level hike to 3.4 miles and the largest of Patjens Lakes. Look for spotted sandpipers flitting about, and bright flowers in the lovely meadow. Reach the third lake at 3.6 miles. An old trail heads to a meadow. Please continue to the right on the new trail.

Climb to 4.7 miles and a well-defined spur trail leading to the Pacific Crest Trail, about 0.2 mile to the east. Cross back out of the wilderness near this point.

At 5.0 miles reach an unmaintained trail, this one leads around Big Lake which is due south. Head left, traveling around the west end of the lake. Come to another junction at 5.5 miles. Both trails lead to the trailhead. The one on the right follows the lake, passing through a free camp area to the trailhead. The trail to the left heads through the trees to the same trailhead at 5.8 miles.

CENTRAL OREGON WILDERNESS AREAS

15 PACIFIC CREST TRAIL
(Includes side trip to Little Belknap Crater)

Distance: 13.1 miles (one-way)
Elevation gain: 2,257 feet; loss 1,621 feet
High point: 6,305 feet
Usually open: July through October
Topographic map: The Mt. Washington
　　　　　　　　　Wilderness Map
Obtain map from: Deschutes National
　　　　　　　　　Forest, Willamette
　　　　　　　　　National Forest

The Pacific Crest Trail (PCT) stretches 2,600 miles from Mexico to Canada, leaving its mark through nearly 13 miles of Mt. Washington Wilderness. The trail is a busy one, especially near the south end of the preserve, but it'll be enjoyed by all who come, especially those visiting during the weekdays. There are magnificent high mountain peaks to see and climb, immense lava flows to explore, and you'll hike through a variety of landscapes, including forest, meadows and lava.

You can begin your hike at either end of the Wilderness. In fact, if you begin at the south end and have a shuttle waiting at the north end, you'll save yourself over 600 feet of climbing. If you intend to do so, just read the following directions in reverse. Long distance hikers may want to hike the trail in both directions, chalking up a 26.2-mile journey by days end. Backpackers will find plenty of campsites along the route, although none sit near a good water source. Our shuttle transported us to Big Lake so our trip began at the north end.

To reach the PCT trailhead near Big Lake, travel via U.S. Hwy. 20, to Big Lake Road (FS Road No. 2690), located 21 miles west of Sisters. From the main highway, turn left (south) onto Road No. 2690 and left again on FS Road No. 811, 3.2 miles away. (Those interested in camping in a developed campground should continue another 0.2 mile on Road No. 2690 to the Big Lake Campground.) Drive Road No. 811 for 0.5 mile where you'll find plenty of room to park. You'll also discover plenty of free places to camp along the road as well.

(The McKenzie Pass PCT Trailhead is located off Oregon Hwy. 242 which is closed during the winter months. Check with the Forest Service for opening dates each year: It usually opens sometime in June or July. The trailhead is located 26 miles east of McKenzie Bridge, 15 miles west of Sisters.)

Back at the north end, head south on the PCT. A sign states this is Trail No. 2007. Actually, it is No. 2000. Pass a wilderness sign 75 yards to the south.

The trail heads out at a level to gradual grade, traveling through a thick forest of lodgepole pine, hemlock, and white pine. Bear grass comforts the fragile ground in July.

At 1.5 miles see Three Fingered Jack through the trees to the north. Farther on, at 2.0 miles, reach a junction to Big Lake. The lake is located about 0.2 mile via the unmaintained trail to the west.

As you climb, notice the change in scenery. Soon, you'll find scattered ferns and high alpine trees. Begin a moderate climb at 2.6 miles.

The grade lessens upon reaching another trail junction at 2.9 miles. A rock cairn and orange flag mark an unmaintained trail to the top of Mt. Washington. The Forest Service says it's approximately two miles to the summit. An eight year old boy climbed the mountain the day we were there. Climbing with his Dad, the boy free climbed to the summit. Bagging this pointed peak, however, isn't for the faint at heart. The Forest Service suggests using a rope: rock on the mountain is rotten and could break away very easily. Most classify this a technical climb.

The trail is moderate to 3.2 miles with a meadow on the right. There's a good view to the southwest at this point. Now the trail travels at a level grade, past lupines and several other species of wildflowers.

You'll find a spring at 3.3 miles. Someone placed an old rusty barrel around the spring and the water looks unlike anything I'd ever want to drink. A nearby water hole is filled with leeches. The Forest Service plans on removing the barrel sometime in the future. It's best to carry water on this hike. The spring sits in a small meadow with Mt. Washington towering overhead. You'll find several old campsites located in the trees on the opposite side of the trail.

Climb a gradual to moderate grade to 4.1

miles and a good view to the north of Three Fingered Jack, Mt. Jefferson, Big Lake, the Hoodoo Ski Area and flat-topped Hayrick Butte. Continue, passing more lupine, scarlet gilia and bear grass, in addition to an old burn site where snags now rule, at 4.3 miles. Look for deer grazing on the grassy slopes.

The soft dirt trail leads to another meadow at 4.9 miles and another view of Mt. Washington. Also, notice the immense lava flow, North and Middle Sisters, Diamond Peak, Scott Mountain and Belknap Crater as you hike the open slope.

The trail angles to the east now as you hike towards Mt. Washington, leveling off and heading back into the trees and an occasional meadow. Begin a gradual descent shortly thereafter, reaching a large flat area (good for camping) off to the left in the trees at 5.8 miles.

Now the trail is a series of gradual ups and downs then a final moderate descent to the end of a lava flow at 7.9 miles. There are several campsites in the area.

The scenery changes dramatically as you hike across lava with hardy trees scattered about, providing little shade. Go around the flow, heading to the southwest and up a gradual to moderate slope. You'll have many views of Mt. Washington along the way. Looking to the east, you'll see Black Butte and the high desert of eastern Oregon.

At 9.5 miles enter the trees again, climbing moderately to a crest at 10.0 miles. Now level off, reaching a huge lava flow at 10.3 miles. From here to the trailhead, the trail consists mostly of sharp, jagged lava. (Please note: The lava is very hard on your pet's feet.) Little grows among the black rock. Look for an occasional pine, some low-lying wildflowers, and old snags.

Reach a junction to Little Belknap Crater at 10.6 miles. A 0.2 mile trail heads to the left at a gradual grade then climbs at a steep grade for the last 50 feet or so. There's a 360 degree view from atop the crater. You'll see Mt. Washington, Three Fingered Jack and Mt. Jefferson to the north. North and Middle Sisters, the Husband, and Diamond Peak to the south. Also, see Mt. Washington Wilderness points of interest such as nearby Belknap Crater and Scott Mountain.

Back at the junction, now at 11.0 miles (it's a 0.4 mile round-trip to the crater), continue down at a gradual to moderate grade to the end of the lava flow at 12.5 miles. Hike on a dirt trail now, skirting along the edge of a lonely tree island bobbing in a sea of lava. Hike over one other small patch of lava before reaching the McKenzie Pass PCT trailhead at 13.1 miles.

Mt. Washington from the PCT trail

16 HAND LAKE

Distance: 1.5 miles (one-way)
Elevation gain: 0 feet; loss 30 feet
High point: 4,800 feet
Usually open: July through October
Topographic map: The Mt. Washington
Wilderness Map
Obtain map from: Deschutes National
Forest, Willamette
National Forest

Hikers often choose hikes that intensify in beauty as they walk along the trail. Perhaps they'll begin at a nondescript trailhead, traveling to a highly scenic lake, or maybe they'll end their hike atop a high, alpine peak where views are many. But this hike is one of those special hikes that begins beset by beauty and ends in similar surroundings. (A few words of caution: This trail is busy during the weekends. Hike during the week if possible. Also, the area is known for it's heavy concentration of blood-sucking mosquitoes early in the season. Wait until mid-August for some relief.)

To reach the trailhead from McKenzie Bridge, a small one market, one gas station, one restaurant and one motel town, drive east on Oregon Hwy. 126. At 4.8 miles reach the junction of Oregon Hwy. 126 and Oregon Hwy. 242. Turn right on Hwy. 242, a narrow paved highway closed during the winter months. (The road usually opens sometime in June or July. Check with the Forest Service for opening dates each year.) Travel trailers are not recommended. Trucks, trailers and motor homes more than a combined length of 50 feet are prohibited.

Climb the windy road, traveling 15.9 miles to FS Road No. 26, the turnoff for Scott Lake. Drive the gravel road for 0.9 mile to the trailhead at picturesque Scott Lake.

There are many fine walk-in campsites at the lake. (Roads around the lake were closed due to heavy use and lakeshore destruction.) Those spots at the north end of the lake come with a wonderful view of the Three Sisters. Grassy meadows, bear grass, and other wildflowers line much of the shoreline.

To reach Hand Lake from the trailhead, head right on Hand Lake Cutoff Trail No. 3513A, now hiking a barricaded dirt road.

Walk past many fine campsites to an extension of Scott Lake at 0.2 mile. Now the trail turns into a regular dirt trail and leads through an occasional meadow, but stays mostly in the trees. At 0.5 mile, you'll encounter the only decline along the route, a steep, but very short descent of about 30 feet.

Enter a large, long meadow after traveling 1.2 miles. Notice Mt. Washington, the area's namesake sitting directly behind Hand Lake. Also, you'll see a giant lava flow which serves as the northern lake boundary. We wondered if the lava flow formed the lake, but a Forest Service employee claims it was already a glacier lake. The lava just happened to flow to this point and stop. But a Forest Service publication claims, "Hand Lake was formed when a tongue of lava from the Twin Craters dammed the outlet."

Reach a shelter at 1.4 miles. Also, you'll see a junction sign nearby. A trail leads to the right at 0.5 mile and back to Hwy. 242. Those wanting a shorter route to Hand Lake may prefer this route, however they'll miss out on pretty Scott Lake. From the Scott Lake turnoff, the trailhead is 1.1 miles farther east on Hwy. 242. The trail is on the left side of the road, parking on the right.

Although shown on the current wilderness map, another trail leading around the west side of the lake to Bunchgrass Ridge does not exist even though the sign reads so. The Forest Service says a loop trail, tying in with the trail to Scott Mountain (See #17, SCOTT MOUNTAIN, for more details), should be completed by 1993.

Walk around Hand Lake, located on the wilderness boundary, for several views of high mountain peaks. You'll see Scott Mountain, North and Middle Sisters. Upon reaching the lake boundary you'll miss seeing Mt. Washington, hidden behind the lava flow.

17 SCOTT MOUNTAIN

Distance: 4.0 miles (one-way)
Elevation gain: 1,366 feet; loss 50 feet
High point: 6,116 feet
Usually open: July through October
Topographic map: The Mt. Washington Wilderness Map
Obtain map from: Deschutes National Forest, Willamette National Forest

The view from red-topped Scott Mountain is fantastic, nearly too good for the little work necessary to reach the summit. Unbelievably, you'll see Oregon's five highest peaks, Mt. Hood, Mt. Jefferson, and the Three—North, Middle and South Sisters. In addition, you'll pass rock-lined wilderness lakes where good fishing and swimming abound. Also, the trail begins at lovely Scott Lake, worth a trip in itself.

To reach the trailhead from McKenzie Bridge, a small town with a market, gas station, restaurant and motel, drive east on Oregon Hwy. 126. At 4.8 miles reach the junction of Oregon Hwy. 126 and Oregon Hwy. 242. Turn right on Hwy. 242, a narrow paved highway closed during the winter months. (Check with the Forest Service for opening dates, usually sometime in June or July.) Travel trailers are not recommended. Trucks, trailers and motorhomes more than a combined length of 50 feet are prohibited.

Climb the windy road, traveling 15.9 miles to FS Road No. 26, the turnoff for Scott Lake. Drive the gravel road for 0.9 mile to the trailhead at picturesque Scott Lake.

There are many splendid walk-in campsites at the lake. (Vehicles are not allowed near the lakeshore due to habitat destruction.) Those sites at the north end of the lake arc especially beautiful. They deliver a wonderful view of the Three Sisters. Grassy meadows, bear grass, and other wildflowers line much of the shoreline. The lake and surrounding trails get a lot of use during the weekends. Visit during the week for a more enjoyable experience.

From the trailhead, hike Benson Trail No. 3502, traveling through the trees, and up at a gradual grade. Bear grass, huckleberry bushes, and occasional lupine stand scat-tered about, covering some of the forest floor.

At 1.0 mile cross a small year-round creek and continue to Benson Lake at 1.3 miles. Also, enter the Wilderness at this point. You'll see a campsite near the lake. Do not camp here: this area is in the process of restoration. Choose a site over 100 feet from the lake.

Anglers should note that both brook and rainbow trout inhabit the 24-acre lake. Located at the 5,250-foot level, the lake is 55 feet deep.

Pass several ponds as you make your way north to the turnoff for Tenas Lakes at 2.5 miles. A 0.1 mile trail leads to the largest of the seven rock-lined lakes. The lakes range in size from one to three acres and most, if not all, support a variety of fish. Some provide proper habitat for rainbow trout, others support brook trout.

If you plan on camping, you'll find several nice spots. As you explore the area, you may come upon a high rock wall, dividing two of the lakes. From here you can see Diamond Peak to the south and North Sister when looking east.

Back on Benson Trail, continue past more ponds to the junction of a trail leading to the Knobs (basalt protrusion) at 2.7 miles. Travel another 0.3 mile and the trail grade intensifies, with an occasional steep incline to negotiate. At 3.7 miles you'll come to an unsigned junction. The current wilderness map shows a trail leading to Bunchgrass Ridge, but this trail hasn't been cleared for years and is difficult to find at the moment. The Forest Service plans to complete a loop trail that would lead from here to a point near Twin Craters and back to the trailhead via Hand Lake. (See #16, HAND LAKE, for more information regarding this scenic spot.)

You can walk to the ridge for a good view of Mt. Hood, Mt. Jefferson, Three Fingered Jack and Mt. Washington. Also, you'll see Hoodoo Ski Area, flat-topped Hayrick Butte, Big Lake and more. Continue hiking the trail, climbing at a steep grade through the trees then into the open, through lava to the summit at 4.0 miles. As mentioned previously, the view is spectacular. You'll see nearly all of the Mt. Washington Wilderness, including Belknap Crater, Little Belknap and the Twin Craters, and much of the Three Sisters Wilderness as well. As you sit atop the old lookout, look to the east, then moving only your head look north and then south. You'll see Oregon's five highest peaks and everything between.

View from Scott Mountain

18 ROBINSON LAKE

Distance: 0.3 miles (one-way)
Elevation gain: 30 feet; loss 0 feet
High point: 3950 feet
Usually open: June through November
Topographic map: The Mt. Washington Wilderness Map
Obtain map from: Deschutes National Forest and Willamette National Forest

Located on the wilderness boundary line, Robinson Lake is an easy hike, especially for those with small children. Less than one mile round-trip, it's a perfect trip for those on their first backpack trip. Also, it's great for those who love the idea of rafting or fishing a wilderness lake. Be forewarned however: Robinson Lake is heavily used.

To reach the trailhead from McKenzie Bridge, a small town with a market, gas station, restaurant and motel, drive east on U.S. Hwy. 126. At 4.8 miles reach the junction of U.S. Hwy. 126 and U.S. Hwy. 242. Keep left on Hwy. 126, driving 11.7 miles to Robinson Lake Road No. 2664. Turn right, and drive until the road ends at the trailhead, 4.4 miles away.

It's a gradual climb through a thick forest of pines to Robinson Lake. Vanilla leaf, huckleberries and a variety of other plants blanket the forest floor. At 0.2 mile reach a junction. Head left 0.1 mile to Robinson Lake. There's a nice camp located about 100 feet from the five acre lake. Other potential sites are available.

Those interested in fishing should note that the 18 foot deep lake is stocked with brook trout.

Old Snag

Along Rock Creek

INTRODUCTION TO THE ROCK CREEK WILDERNESS

Rock Creek is one of Oregon's least visited wilderness areas and for good reason. There are no trails, nor will there ever be.

The 7,386 acre preserve stretches from sea level at the mighty Pacific to 2200 feet atop a ridge near the center of the Wilderness. The Siuslaw National Forest manages the area.

As in the other two Siuslaw Wilderness Areas, horse travel is not allowed. The reason is the same—fragile terrain.

The preserve was designated wilderness in 1984 with the signing of the Oregon Wilderness Act. Surrounded by roads, the Rock Creek area was never harvested, nor were roads built through it. Fortunately the land consists of some low value hardwoods and immature conifer stands.

If you could hike deep into the region, beginning at the ocean, you'd walk under Sitka spruce and western hemlock for the first two miles. From this point, you'd see the forest gradually shift to old-growth Douglas fir and hemlock. Dense undergrowth nearly smothers the forest floor. Plant species include salal, sword fern and salmonberry. Rhododendrons bloom in May. Alder, bigleaf maple, and vine maple line the creeks. Wildflowers flourish in the spring. Look for candyflowers, monkeyflowers, asters, and foxglove to name a few.

The preserve rests 15 miles north of Florence and as with the other coast areas, receives a substantial amount of rain. Sixty to eighty inches fall each year. Fog blankets the coast and valleys most of the summer. Winters are usually free of snow. Spring and fall are perhaps the best times for clear sunny days.

Hardy pioneers are known to have tried homesteading within the boundaries of what is now known as the Rock Creek Wilderness. Three homesteads once existed: two on upper Big Creek and the third on lower Rock Creek. The lower Rock Creek homestead sat a short distance above the present-day Rock Creek Forest Camp. Homesteaders lived there until the mid-1940's.

Two primary creeks, Rock Creek and Big Creek, flow through the area, both draining directly into the Pacific. Both streams support runs of anadromous fish.

For more information contact:

Forest Supervisor
Waldport Ranger District
P.O. Box 400
Waldport, OR. 97394
(503) 563-3211

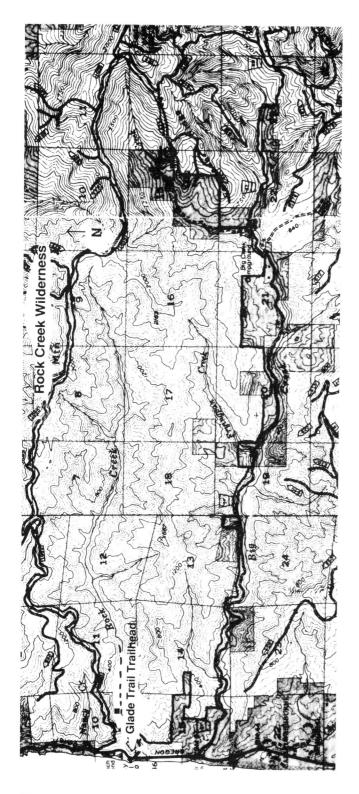

CENTRAL OREGON WILDERNESS AREAS

19 ROCK CREEK TRAIL

Distance: 1.0 mile (one-way)
Elevation gain: 40 feet; loss 20 feet
High point: 180 feet
Usually open: Year round
Topographic map: U.S.G.S. Heceta Head, Oregon
Obtain map from: U.S.G.S.—Denver, CO.

For convenience's sake I've named the following the Rock Creek Trail although one doesn't really exist. Well, there is a trail but it isn't maintained and will never be for this is a trailless wilderness. This is most likely an old game trail and an occasional hiker keeps it from going back to its natural state.

To reach the trailhead, located at Rock Creek Forest Campground, travel U.S. Hwy. 101, 10.6 miles south from Yachats. Yachats is a scenic coast town with all the amenities. Turn east at the sign pointing the way to the "Rock Creek Campground" via FS Road No. 514.

The campground is open only during the summer months, from May 25 through September 15. There's a 10-day stay limit. For a fee, you'll find fire grates, picnic tables, restrooms and water. (Do not plan on staying at Big Creek Campground, shown on the map and located in the southeast portion of the area. It was removed after wilderness designation.)

We visited the area in the early spring, parked at the locked gate, located off Hwy. 101, and walked in a half mile, thus the total of one mile for this trail. It's an easy walk along the creek and through the campground to site number 16, starting point for the Rock Creek Trail.

Follow the unmaintained trail as it winds along the north end of the creek. The trail runs for another 0.5 mile and leads to a pretty meadow after crossing the creek, which you'll have to ford. The water is usually a chilly 56 degrees. In the spring you'll find a variety of flowers, including buttercups, crimson columbine, and huge skunk cabbage.

While viewing the creek, look for the American Dipper, a robin-size brown bird that walks underwater while looking for its prey.

Fern in the Rock Creek Wilderness

INTRODUCTION TO THE THREE SISTERS WILDERNESS

Lofty mountain peaks search for the heavens in the Three Sisters Wilderness. Mighty pines stand tall, swaying in the breeze. In the summer, squirrels scamper about, chattering all the while. Clear blue liquid waterways begin near age-old glaciers, trickling first then streaming down, fast becoming a creek or river. More than 350 azure lakes dot the land like jewels and flowers carpet the landscape. Backpackers flock to the area for this is Oregon's busiest wilderness area.

Fall arrives. Wild animals migrate down into the warmer valleys below. Those that remain store food for the winter or put on fat to help them through the lean days ahead. The wind blows, nights are downright frosty: few people venture into the Wilderness.

Soon the winter snows arrive. Cross-country skiers come to enjoy the solitude of a crisp winter day. Snowshoers shuffle through the forest. Others, too cold to venture outside, stay at home by the fireplace, dreaming of spring.

The days are noticeably longer, the sun more intense as spring approaches. The snow slowly melts away, carving a path to a dirt trail below. Mosquitoes hatch, their sole purpose to make life miserable for outdoor people (or so it seems). Birds sing. It's nearly time to explore the Three Sisters Wilderness once again.

The Three Sisters, once named Faith, Hope, and Charity, by pioneer missionaries, and the mountains for which the Wilderness was named, dominate the landscape. In the mid-1800s, weary travelers used them as pilot-peaks to steer them over the rugged inland plateau. Today, they still attract travelers, but these are outdoor enthusiasts looking for fun and relaxation.

Hiking, fishing, backpacking, mountain climbing, photography, wildlife and wildflower viewing are possible in this Central Oregon Cascade Wilderness.

Ranging from a low of 1,850 feet to a high of 10,358 feet, the preserve is located in and managed by both the Willamette and Deschutes National Forests. The Wilderness first gained protection in 1937. Established as a Primitive Area, it was later reclassified as wilderness in 1957. In 1964, it became part of the Congressionally-established National Wilderness Preservation System.

There are approximately 280 miles of trail within the 34-mile long, 280,500-acre preserve. The Pacific Crest National Scenic Trail, known as the PCT, traverses the Wilderness for roughly 42 miles.

Trails lead through varied terrain. Most begin in dense forests of Douglas fir on the western slopes of the Cascades and ponderosa pine on the eastern slopes. Hikers pass through western white pine, Engelmann spruce, white fir, western red cedar, and western hemlock as well. Mountain hemlock, lodgepole pine, alpine fir, and whitebark pine cover the higher elevations.

Flowers blanket numerous meadows during the brief summer months. Melted snow feeds blue lupine, red Indian paintbrush, heather, arnica, larkspur, bluebells, wild sunflowers, avalanche lily, elephant head, and countless others.

Tall mountain peaks command attention in the preserve. From atop 10,358 foot South Sister, Oregon's third highest peak, hikers enjoy a summit crater filled with snow and ice most of the year. During a warm spell, the ice melts and like magic, an aqua-blue lake appears. At 10,200 feet, Oregon's highest lake tempts hikers to take an icy dip.

"Shorter" peaks are visible from South Sisters summit. See Middle Sister (10,053 feet), and North Sister (10,094 feet) to the north. On a clear day, Washington's Mount Rainer, an amazing 180 miles distant, is visible as well. In between the Sisters and Mount Rainer, view Three Fingered Jack, Mount Washington, Mount Jefferson and Mount Hood, Oregon's highest peak. To the east see Bachelor Butte, and within the Wilderness itself, see many other peaks surrounding South Sister.

Broken Top, a unique 9,175 foot peak, rests close to South Sister. For an "inside view" of a volcano, recreationists should examine this mountain. See how a volcano is formed while viewing layers of pumice, bombs, basalt blocks, layers of pumice, and lava flows.

Although named the Three Sisters, researchers believe they are by no means "sisters." Some say the label should read the "Mother and Two Daughters" for the North Sister is much older than the Middle and South Sisters. South Sister is by far the baby of the three mountains.

Sixteen glaciers rest, as they have for millions of years, on the slopes of four major mountains in the Three Sisters Wilderness. Today, however, the glaciers have diminished considerably. At one time they covered the mountains down to their 4,000 foot bases.

If you're hiking on a windy day, look for "smoke clouds." When the wind is whipping around, portions of pulverized rock, known as rock flour, gather up from the glacier. Swirling around, they look like smoke clouds over the mountains. The dust sinks into nearby streams, turning them milky-white.

You'll see evidence of glacial activity throughout the preserve. Explore the 2300-year old pumice flows at Rock Mesa. Hike through rugged lava flows at Oppie Dildock Pass, or to Linton Lake, formed when a lava flow fashioned a dam across Linton Creek.

Mountain climbing is popular here. All the Sisters attract climbers and, remarkably, some ascend all three peaks in one day. (The Forest Service describes access routes in the Forest Service sheet, "The Sisters Group of the High Cascades," available at no charge.)

Both expert mountaineers and school children climb South Sister. The north and east slopes are challenging to say the least. The southern route, however, is but one long climb. (See #28, Moraine Lake to South Sister for more details on this climb.)

Climbing mountains is challenging and dangerous. Unfortunately, accidents are a fairly common occurrence. The Forest Service warns that rescue teams are rarely able to reach an accident victim in less than 6 to 12 hours. Sometimes, rescue attempts may take more than 24 hours.

To ensure a safe trip, never climb alone. The Forest Service recommends a party of no less than three or four people, one of whom has previously climbed the peak or is a competent mountaineer. All climbers should carry and know how to use mountaineering equipment.

Wear proper clothing, including good lugged boots. Wear sunglasses as well and bring sun protection. Always carry extra high energy food along and leave word with someone back home as to your whereabouts and expected time of return.

Green Lakes is a popular base camp for mountain climbers and is favored among hikers and backpackers as well. Three lakes (one medium-sized and two small) sit in between Broken Top and South Sister, all providing a fantastic view of the surrounding peaks from the 6500-foot level.

Whether climbing mountains, picnicking under a shady pine, or sauntering along the trail, you may see a variety of animal life. Columbia black-tailed deer, mule deer, Roosevelt elk, and black bear are common. Cougar inhabitat the area as well. Many small animals make their home here. These include mink, marten, raccoon, porcupine, bobcat, weasel, and coyote.

Bird life includes blue and ruff grouse, the principal game birds living in the Wilderness. Bald eagles swoop down, fetching fish out of some of the lakes.

There are many excellent fishing areas in the Three Sisters Wilderness. When possible, the Oregon Department of Fish and Wildlife stocks many of the lakes. State regulations (licenses, seasons and bag limits) apply when fishing in the preserve. Anglers may hook eastern brook, rainbow, and cutthroat trout.

Beginning in the summer of 1991, a free wilderness permit is required. Check with a District Ranger office for more information.

For more information contact:

Forest Supervisor	or	Forest Supervisor
Deschutes National Forest		Willamette National Forest
211 N.E. Revere Street		P.O. Box 1607
Bend, Oregon 97701		Eugene Federal Building
		Eugene, Oregon 97440

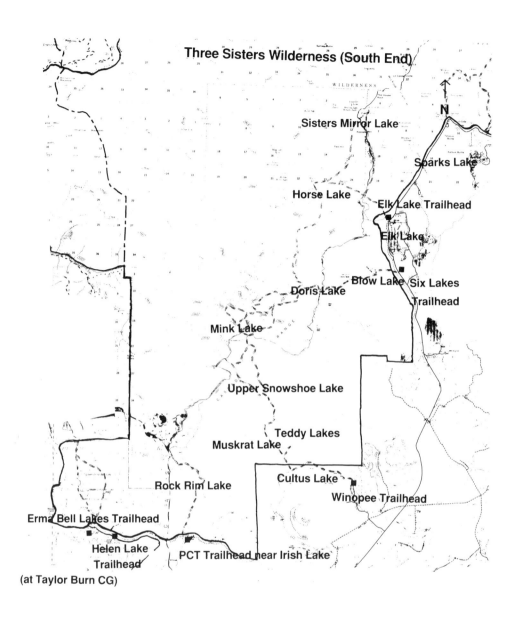

Three Sisters Wilderness (South End)

N

Sisters Mirror Lake

Sparks Lake

Horse Lake

Elk Lake Trailhead

Elk Lake

Blow Lake   Six Lakes

Doris Lake   Trailhead

Mink Lake

Upper Snowshoe Lake

Teddy Lakes

Muskrat Lake

Cultus Lake

Rock Rim Lake   Winopee Trailhead

Erma Bell Lakes Trailhead

Helen Lake
Trailhead   PCT Trailhead near Irish Lake

(at Taylor Burn CG)

CENTRAL OREGON WILDERNESS AREAS

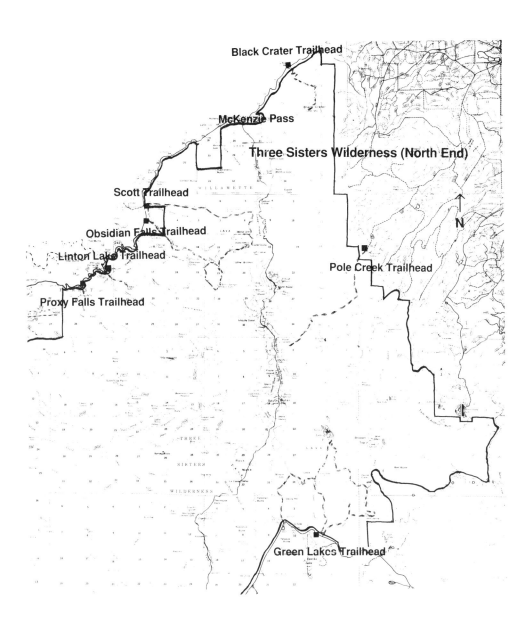

Black Crater Trailhead

McKenzie Pass

Three Sisters Wilderness (North End)

Scott Trailhead

Obsidian Falls Trailhead

Linton Lake Trailhead

Pole Creek Trailhead

Proxy Falls Trailhead

N

Green Lakes Trailhead

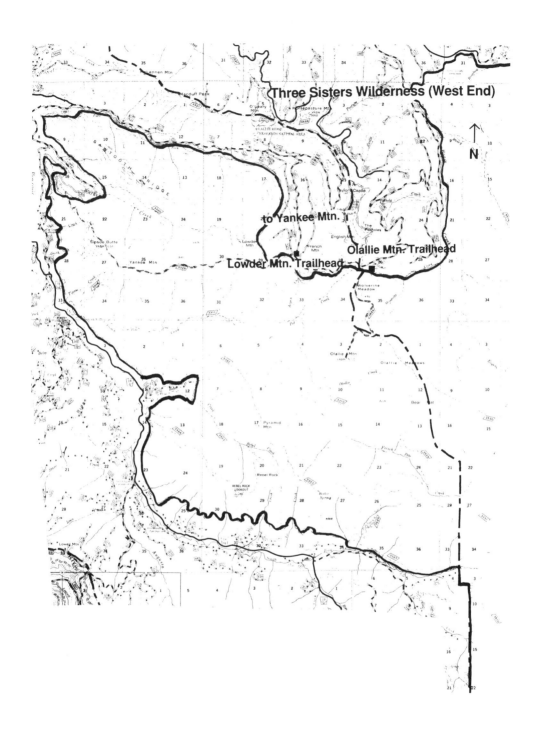

Three Sisters Wilderness (West End)

to Yankee Mtn.

Olallie Mtn. Trailhead

Lowder Mtn. Trailhead

20 ROCK RIM LAKE VIA THE PCT

Distance: 3.7 miles (one-way)
Elevation gain: 500 feet; loss 0 feet
High point: 6,000 feet
Usually open: July through October
Topographic map: The Three Sisters
                  Wilderness Map
Obtain map from: Deschutes National
                  Forest, Willamette
                  National Forest

Rock Rim Lake sits in the southern portion of the Three Sisters Wilderness. A beautiful blue lake, its scenic qualities are well worth the little effort needed to reach it.

To reach the trailhead, drive 24 miles southeast from Oakridge, via Oregon Highway 58. Turn left on paved Waldo Lake Road No. 5897 and drive another 11.1 miles to a fork in the road. Stay left, driving paved FS Road No. 5898 to a junction, 13 miles from Highway 58.

Turn right on paved FS Road No. 515 and drive 0.3 mile to unmaintained FS Road No. 514, now heading towards Taylor Burn. Continue 4.1 miles to a junction. Head right on FS Road No. 600 and reach the Pacific Crest Trail (PCT) trailhead at 0.9 mile. (Both Roads No. 514 and Road No. 600 are unimproved dirt roads: potholes and ruts are common. Trailers are not recommended.)

There are several places to park near the PCT. Also, camping is available at the Irish Lake Campground located about 100 yards farther down the road. Facilities include old pit toilets and picnic tables. Anglers will find the fishing good if fished during the proper time of year.

Head north on the PCT No. 2000 and reach the wilderness boundary sign in 400 feet. Travel along the west side of Irish Lake, passing several potential campsites as you hike through a forest of lodgepole pines and western white pine. At 0.7 mile there is a spur trail leading to the lake.

Head away from the lake now, remaining level or hiking a gradual up and down to Riffle Lake at 1.3 miles. Lily pads dot this small lake. Pass several ponds before reaching Brahma Lake at 2.2 miles. Stretching out across 10 acres, Brahma Lake is stocked with brook trout. Anglers throw in your lines!

The trail forks shortly after reaching the 12-foot deep lake. The PCT continues to the right, and the trail to the left leads along the lake, past several campsites. It meets back with the PCT in 0.1 mile.

Cross several small bridges and a stream, then hike past some mucky ponds before coming to Jezebel Lake at 3.2 miles.

From Jezebel Lake hike through a forest which now includes hemlock, moderately climbing to 3.5 miles and a junction. The PCT continues to the right. Head left on the unsigned trail to Rock Rim Lake at 3.7 miles.

You'll find plenty of campsites at the lake with the east side areas providing a view of the tip of Irish Mountain. At 13 feet deep, the four-acre lake is excellent for swimming. Brook trout reside in the lake. The Forest Service claims the fishing is good.

Red tailed hawk

Rock Rim Lake

21 HELEN LAKE TRAIL

Distance: 0.3 mile (one-way)
Elevation gain: 0 feet; loss 150 feet
High point: 5,500 feet
Usually open: July through October
Topographic map: The Three Sisters
Wilderness Map
Obtain map from: Deschutes National
Forest, Willamette
National Forest

The Helen Lake Trail is a short trail leading to an open lake with rock outcrops lining some of the shore. The whole family will enjoy this excellent day hike.

To reach the trailhead, drive 24 miles southeast from Oakridge, via Oregon Highway 58. Turn left on paved Waldo Lake Road No. 5897 and drive another 11.1 miles to a fork in the road. Stay left, continuing on paved FS Road No. 5898 and reach another junction 13 miles from Hwy. 58.

At this point turn right on paved FS Road No. 515 and drive 0.3 mile to unmaintained FS Road No. 514. Head towards Taylor Burn now, traveling 4.1 miles to a junction. Turn left on FS Road No. 517 and drive 2.4 miles to the trailhead. (Roads No. 514 and 517 are unimproved dirt roads with plenty of ruts and potholes. Trailers are not recommended.) Two parking spots are available.

Begin hiking Helen Lake Trail No. 3577, traveling through lodgepole pines. Gradually descend along the easy-to-follow trail to Helen Lake at 0.3 mile.

Anglers will find the six-acre lake stocked with rainbow trout. Fingerlings are dumped into the lake every other year. Swimmers will find plenty of room for dog-paddling in the 20 foot deep water.

Upper Erma Bell Lake

CENTRAL OREGON WILDERNESS AREAS

22 ERMA BELL/WILLIAM LAKES LOOP

Distance: 7.2 miles (complete loop)
Elevation gain: 900 feet; loss 900 feet
High point: 5,200 feet
Usually open: July through October
Topographic map: The Three Sisters
             Wilderness Map
Obtain map from: Deschutes National
             Forest, Willamette
             National Forest

Snuggled down in the southern tip of the Three Sisters Wilderness, the Erma Bell Lakes consist of three mountain lakes, each one a bit higher in elevation than the other. Upper Erma Bell, Middle Erma Bell, and Lower Erma Bell Lakes are accurately named. Crowds file past these three lakes on summer weekends. The other half of the loop, however, leads to Williams Lake and a chance for solitude.

Two trailheads provide access to the loop. The following guide begins at the Taylor Burn Campground, a central starting point for a variety of trails leading into both the Three Sisters and Waldo Lake Wilderness Areas.

To reach the trailhead, drive 24 miles southeast from Oakridge, via Oregon Highway 58. Turn left on paved Waldo Lake Road No. 5897 and drive another 11.1 miles to a fork in the road. Stay left, continuing on paved FS Road No. 5898 for an additional 1.9 miles to a junction.

At this point turn right towards Taylor Burn, now driving paved FS Road No. 515. Turn right on FS Road No. 514 at 0.3 mile and continue 4.1 miles to a junction. Turn left on FS Road No. 517 and drive 3.2 miles to the trailhead. (Roads No. 514 and 517 are unimproved dirt roads with plenty of ruts and potholes. Trailers are not recommended.)

You'll find the trailhead a hundred yards or so before the Taylor Burn Campground. The shady camp comes complete with picnic tables, fire grates, and pit toilets. It's also free. In addition, spring water is available by walking or driving past the wilderness registration box 100 yards or so to some rocks on the right. Follow the path through the rocks to the spring, located about 75 feet off the road.

The following loop begins here, but those in need of a smoother ride to the trailhead can begin at Skookum Creek Campground. From that point, hike 0.3 mile to catch this loop at the 3.4 miles mark. To reach the Skookum Creek Campground drive from Westfir, located just north of Oakridge. Head up the North Fork Road No. 19 for 32 miles to Box Canyon. Make a sharp right on Skookum Creek Road No. 1957 and head south for about 4 miles to the trailhead and campground.

Back at the Taylor Burn Campground, begin hiking Erma Bell Trail No. 3563. Head north and pass a wilderness boundary sign in 100 feet. Gradually descend through the trees and lush undergrowth to a junction at 0.4 mile.

Proceed left on Erma Bell Trail (this loop returns on the trail to the right) and continue down to Mud Lake at 0.7 mile. There's a spur trail leading to the seven acre lake at 0.8 mile. Anglers needn't cast in their lines for the fishing is poor and campsites are non-existent.

The trail leads through old-growth forest consisting of hemlock and cedar for the most part, with huckleberry, lupine and bear grass blanketing the ground. At 1.0 mile reach the junction of Judy Lake Trail No. 3575. Continue straight to Upper Erma Bell Lake at 1.6 miles. At twenty-five acres, Upper Erma Bell is the smallest of the three lakes, with plenty of campsites available and the fishing is excellent. Rainbow and brook trout inhabit the lake.

At 1.7 miles pass a small pond on the left and at 1.9 miles come to Middle Erma Bell Lake. Middle Erma Bell is the largest of the Erma Bell lakes, spanning 60 acres. Rhododendrons line the lake. See a splendid show of color in mid-June through mid-July when the pink blossoms bloom in profusion. Plentiful campsites and good fishing are found at this 46-foot deep lake.

When camping here and at other lakes throughout the Wilderness, please make note of the restoration sites in progress and camp elsewhere. Hikers have trampled the vegetation surrounding many of the most popular lakes in the Wilderness. Currently, it is in the restoration process. Several campsites have been roped off and signs ask that you do not camp or walk through these areas. Please obey the posted signs and allow the vegetation to grow again.

At 2.1 and 2.2 miles there are short trails leading down to Middle Erma Bell Lake and campsites are available as well. Also, there's a small waterfall at 2.2 miles, the water flowing from Middle Erma Bell Lake to Lower Erma Bell Lake which is visible now.

Continue down at a gradual rate to 2.4 miles and another spur trail leading to a restoration area. Directly across from the spur, look for a trail heading in the opposite direction. This trail leads to a nice camp located about 50 feet up the hill.

Proceed to 2.5 miles, cross a bridge, and see a variety of trails leading up to camps along the north shore of Lower Erma Bell Lake. Reaching to a depth of 60 feet, Lower Erma Bell Lake is the deepest of the three lakes and has rainbow trout living in its waters. The fishing rates a "very good."

Continue down along the trail—which has progressively become wider—to a junction at 3.4 miles. Skookum Creek Campground is to the left about 0.3 mile. Turn right to complete the loop, now hiking Irish Mountain Trail No. 3588.

The trail leads up, then down to Otter Lake located at 3.8 miles. This area is also in the restoration process although there are two or three camp areas available. Some type of red lily pad blankets a large portion of the lake. Also, rhododendrons border some of the trail. Anglers will find "good" fishing with brook trout found in the 17 acre lake.

At 4.0 miles cross the outflow creek (camp nearby) and reach a junction at 4.1 miles. Now hike Williams Lake Trail No. 3589, heading up at a moderate grade then level to a meadow at 4.4 miles. At times the trail is a bit difficult to follow, but blazed trees lead the way and finding the trail shouldn't be a problem. During the early summer months you'll find, among other species, columbine, lilies, and lupine.

Gradually climb again, hiking past bear grass, huckleberries, and more lupine. At 5.2 and 5.4 miles cross streams, hiking level now. Travel a gradual up and down to 6.2 miles and the smallest of the two Williams Lakes. Reach the largest of the Williams Lakes in another 0.1 mile.

There are at least two camps at Williams Lakes. Lodgepole pine and western white pine surround the brook-filled lake.

To complete the loop head into the trees, crossing a meadow and gradually climbing to 6.7 and the Erma Bell Lakes Junction. Turn left and proceed back to the trailhead at 7.2 miles.

23 SISTERS MIRROR/ HORSE LAKE LOOP

Distance: 12.5 miles (complete loop)
Elevation gain: 1,800 feet; loss 1,800 feet
High point: 6,520 feet
Usually open: July through October
Topographic map: The Three Sisters Wilderness Map
Obtain map from: Deschutes National Forest, Willamette National Forest

If variety is, as they say, "the spice of life," then you're bound to do a lot of living on this loop. Hike through dense forest where little more than dwarf huckleberry grow on the forest floor. Or climb to the top of Koosah Mountain for a fantastic view of surrounding Cascade peaks. Of course, there's also the chance to swim or fish in a variety of lakes.

To reach the trailhead near Elk Lake, drive 33 miles west of Bend, via the Cascades Lakes Highway (Oregon Hwy. 46). Turn right at the Elk Lake Trailhead sign and continue 0.2 mile on a paved road, then park in a large dirt parking area. A pit toilet is located at the trailhead.

To begin the loop, stay on Horse Lake Trail upon reaching a junction to Island Meadow Trail just 200 feet from the trailhead (this will be your return trail). Hike through lodgepole pine, western white pine, and mountain hemlock as you head up to the Wilderness boundary at 0.1 mile.

Continue, reaching another junction (Quinn Meadow Horse Camp) at 0.3 mile. Proceed straight at a gradual to moderate grade to 1.4 miles and the Pacific Crest Trail (PCT). Turn right onto the PCT, now heading north to Sisters Mirror Lake.

As you climb the slope, you won't see much except trees until the 3.3 miles mark. At this point, you'll see Diamond Peak to the south. View Red Hill to the southwest at 3.5 miles.

Mountain hemlock dominate as you begin to switchback up at 3.7 miles, then wind around to the east and up to the top of Koosah Mountain. From this high point at 6,520 feet, you'll see (to the north and east) South Sister, Broken Top, and Mt. Bachelor. To the south see Diamond Peak and Mount

Thielsen. Lakes visible include Elk, Lava, and Crane Prairie Lakes.

From the top, head down at a moderate grade, hiking switchbacks with more views of South Sister along the way. Reach a junction at 5.4 miles.

Sisters Mirror Lake is to the right of the junction, a few hundred yards down the trail. Or, you can walk the fishing trail around the lake directly in front of you, walking the east side of the lake to Sisters Mirror Lake.

As you may have guessed, there is a view of South Sister from Sisters Mirror Lake, but you won't find the whole mountain mirrored there. Instead, the top of the mountain provides a splendid backdrop to Sisters Mirror Lake.

Besides Sisters Mirror, there are many small lakes in the area. The fishing is reportedly good at all of these, with most stocked with brook trout and some with rainbow trout as well. Campsites are abundant. Please stay away from wilderness restoration areas, however.

Wildflower lovers should visit this area in early summer when a variety of flowers carpet the meadows surrounding some of the lakes. Also, there are several meadows farther along this loop trail, all filled with flowers during the proper season.

To continue the loop, head southwest from the junction towards Horse Lake, hiking a nearly level trail past several small lakes to 6.0 miles. Begin a gradual to moderate downhill at this point to 8.4 miles and a junction. Proceed to the right another 0.2 mile to the Horse Lake junction. Trails at this point lead to Dumbell Lake, Horse Creek Trailhead, and the middle trail leads to Horse Lake in 0.1 mile.

There are plenty of campsites around the 60 acre lake, some (on the south and west sides) with a good view of Mount Bachelor and South Sister. At 24 feet deep, the lake is perfect for swimming, and anglers will find brook trout living in it.

Back at the trailhead, turn right, heading south towards Dumbell Lake. Cross a creek at 8.7 miles (the only fresh water on this loop) and notice two camps nearby. Angle up to the left from the creek and reach a junction in 200 feet. Head straight (south) following a sign to Dumbell Lake. Proceed to another junction at 9.1 miles.

Now follow the sign to the left and up to

Sunset Lake, a gradual climb which passes by the north end of the lake. Several spur trails lead to the 40 acre lake, where rainbow trout may be found.

Pass three ponds as you hike to a meadow at 10.4 miles. Cross the meadow and reach a junction as you re-enter the woods. Stay straight, now hiking the PCT. A sign points the way to Sisters Mirror Lake.

The terrain is a series of ups and downs as you pass a large meadow on your right, then it's down a gradual to moderate grade to a junction at 11.5 miles. Stay straight, hiking down to the Wilderness boundary at 12.3 miles, and back to the trailhead at 12.5 miles.

Broken Top at dawn

CENTRAL OREGON WILDERNESS AREAS

24 BROKEN TOP/ GREEN LAKES LOOP

Distance: 10.8 miles (complete loop)
Elevation gain: 1,460 feet; loss 1,460 feet
High point: 6,880 feet
Usually open: July through October
Topographic map: The Three Sisters
Wilderness Map
Obtain map from: Deschutes National
Forest, Willamette
National Forest

Folks with solitude on the agenda shouldn't hike into the Green Lakes area. Crowds fill the Green Lakes Basin on summer weekends and holidays; weekdays are seldom free of crowds as well. But upon hiking this loop we were able to see why people flock to the area. It's absolutely stunning!

From the Broken Top Trail there are excellent views of Broken Top. Hike across fragile alpine areas where stunted trees litter the land and tiny flowers struggle to grow. Along this portion of the loop you'll see less people than at the Green Lakes area. Located on a 6500-foot saddle between South Sister and Broken Top, the Green Lakes Basin is a beautiful spot with excellent views, and access to climbing South Sister, Oregon's third highest peak.

To reach the Green Lakes trailhead drive west from Bend, via the Cascades Lakes Highway (Oregon Highway No. 46) for 27 miles. Park in the large parking area located across the road from Sparks Lake. Pit toilets are provided for your convenience. Also, a horse ramp is available.

This loop begins by hiking the Soda Creek Trail, located on the northeast side of the parking area. Because you'll see less people on the first half of the loop, you may want to hike to the Broken Top Trail and then back, thus avoiding the hordes who are probably hiking the Green Lakes Trail. But that decision is up to you.

Another good alternative for small children or adults who aren't into hiking uphill is to drive to the Broken Top Trail via FS Road No. 200, a bumpy, sometimes impassable dirt road. Hike down the Broken Top Trail at a gradual grade from the road.

Soda Creek Trail leads past the wilderness boundary sign at 0.1 mile, heading nearly level through a forest of lodgepole pine and an occasional mountain hemlock. Reach Soda Creek Meadow at 1.5 miles. Skirt the west side of the meadow for 150 yards or so and cross a creek via a log bridge.

Now hike up at a moderate rate through dense forest to a switchback at 2.5 miles. Head up, then out across a flower-covered open slope where a lone lodgepole pops up now and again. There's a good view of Sparks Lake and the surrounding area from this point.

For the next mile you'll head in and out of the trees, crossing open slopes while hiking to Crater Creek and a terrific view of Broken Top at 3.3 miles. Follow wood markers across the open alpine areas to a junction at 3.5 miles. Monkey flowers and paintbrush line Crater Creek with many other species in evidence.

If you intend to camp in this area, please do not place your tent or belongings on the fragile vegetation. Instead try camping in the trees to the east. Established camps are easy to find.

At the junction the trail to the right heads to Todd Lake. Turn left to reach the Broken Top Trail. Cross Crater Creek and once again follow the wood markers up at a moderate grade to 4.2 miles and the Broken Top Trail.

Although the loop continues to the left, a delightful side trip awaits those hiking to the east (right) for 1.8 miles. (A sign points the way to "Crater Ditch Trailhead - 1.2 miles," but the sign isn't accurate. It's 0.6 mile farther.)

Spectacular views of Broken Top are possible from the trail, as well as close-up views of reddish-colored Ball Butte. In addition, you can hike up the creek to the east of Ball Butte and on up to one of the highest of Broken Top's many peaks. As you hike up the creek you'll also have a good view of Tam McArthur Rim, located to the northeast. Water and campsites are plentiful from here to FS Road No. 200 where the Broken Top Trail ends.

To continue the loop, head left (west) at the junction, hiking a gradual up and down across a mostly open slope dotted with mountain hemlock and various other species. At 4.9 miles there is a fantastic view of South Sister and the west side of Broken Top. Now the trail is nearly level until you cross a creek at 5.3 miles.

Hike up a short, steep slope then descend gradually. Now travel through the trees for the most part to 5.7 miles and a view of the North Sister. Continue down to a creek at 6.4 miles, and at 6.5 miles a breathtaking view of two of the three Green Lakes, South Sister, and Broken Top.

Trails lead throughout this heavily-used area, past numerous campsites, and then north a mile or so to the northernmost of the three Green Lakes, a 10 acre lake stocked with both brook and rainbow trout.

White pumice blankets much of the area with a scattering of fragile alpine flowers during the summer months. Clumps of trees dot the terrain. Because trees are scarce, fires are prohibited within one mile of the Green Lakes Basin. Failure to abide by the rules could result in a $500.00 fine and up to 6 months in jail.

On a clear and calm day, hikers see the nearby peaks mirrored in the still waters of the Green Lakes, a favorite area for photographers. Folks interested in swimming will find plenty of opportunities as the lakes range from 25 feet to 79 feet deep. The largest of the chain—Middle Green Lake—spans 85 acres and is stocked with brook and rainbow trout. Rainbow trout and cutthroat trout live in South Green Lake.

When visiting the Green Lakes Basin you'll undoubtedly see hardy souls climbing South Sister or Broken Top. The most popular route up South Sister heads up the southeast slope, south of Lewis Glacier, then up the south ridge. Another route, from Moraine Lake, is also popular and leads to the 10,358 foot summit. (See #28 MORAINE LAKE TO SOUTH SISTER for more details.) At 9,165 feet, Broken Top is also a favorite climb. (For more information on climbing the Three Sisters and Broken Top ask Forest Service personnel for the information sheets entitled, "The Sisters Group of the High Cascades.")

The loop continues by hiking straight ahead to a junction at 6.7 miles. Turn left at the junction towards the Green Lakes Trailhead. (Reach Middle and North Green Lakes by hiking to the right towards Park Meadows.)

The trail now heads down at a gradual decline, following scenic Fall Creek (the fishing is reportedly fair) and the Newberry Flow, a large lava flow. Hike mainly in the open, then through the trees and down a series of switchbacks beginning at 7.5 miles and back down along the creek.

At 8.3 miles cross Fall Creek and cross another creek in a few hundred yards. Both crossings are by bridge. Reach a junction to Moraine Lake Trail at 8.6 miles. Continue straight and cross back over Fall Creek via bridge at 10.7 miles and head back to the trailhead parking area at 10.8 miles.

Green Lakes and South Sister

25 CULTUS LAKE TO UPPER SNOWSHOE LAKE

Distance: 7.6 miles (one-way)
Elevation gain: 320 feet; loss 0 feet
High point: 5,120 feet
Usually open: July through October
Topographic map: The Three Sisters
                 Wilderness Map
Obtain map from: Deschutes National
                 Forest, Willamette
                 National Forest

The Three Sisters Wilderness consists of fragile alpine slopes, rugged lava flows, tall peaks, and forest land dotted with numerous lakes. This trail leads through the latter: tall pines, and several lakes, most good for fishing, some good for swimming. Then there is Muskrat Cabin, a swell place to spend a night or two.

To reach the trailhead at Cultus Lake, drive to the junction of the Cascades Lakes Highway (Oregon Highway No. 46) and the Cultus Lake turnoff (FS Road No. 4635). Head west on Road No. 4635, driving the paved road to gravel FS Road No. 100 at 2.1 miles. (Stay to the right when you reach a fork to Winopee Trailhead at 1.8 miles.) Follow the gravel road to another fork at 0.5 mile. Head left via a dusty dirt road for an additional 0.1 mile to the trailhead. You'll find plenty of parking here.

Begin hiking Winopee Trail No. 16 staying straight upon meeting up with a campground trail in 0.1 mile. The trail leads through a forest of primarily lodgepole pine, with an occasional western white pine and ponderosa pine in evidence. Later, you'll see western hemlock, mountain hemlock, and some true fir.

It's a nearly level hike as you skirt along the north edge of Cultus Lake. At 0.9 mile you'll find a sandy beach with plenty of room to camp and a boat ramp for those folks at the campground in need of "getting away from it all."

At 2.4 miles reach a junction to Corral Lakes. Stay straight, following the sign to Deer Lake. Continue to 2.6 miles and another junction. Now head away from the lake and north toward Winopee Lake and the Pacific Crest Trail (PCT).

Enter the Wilderness at 2.9 miles, then climb gradually to 3.2 miles and a junction. Teddy Lakes is located to the east via a level trail.

Teddy Lakes is a good side trip with South Teddy Lake located very near the junction. The Oregon Department of Fish and Wildlife stocks South Teddy Lake with brook trout. The trail ends at North Teddy, the largest of the two Teddy Lakes, 0.5 miles from the junction. There is a camp where the trail ends. Also, you'll find a camp by following a trail 0.4 mile to the left and around to the west end of the lake. Spanning a distance of about 30 acres, the 28 foot deep lake is stocked with rainbow trout.

If you're lucky, you may see osprey fishing the lake. Also, gray jays may decide to invade your camp, begging for a tidbit or two.

From the junction at 3.2 miles, hike through the trees at a nearly level grade to 4.1 miles and a view of Muskrat Lake. At 4.2 miles you'll see a trail leading to Muskrat Cabin, a fine place to visit or spend the night.

Muskrat Cabin was built in 1934. A nonprofit organization, the "Friends of the Muskrat," maintains the cabin. When we visited the cabin it was in excellent condition, very clean, and previous visitors had left a variety of food items. If you have extra food, please leave what you can. Also, you're welcome to take any food you might need.

Although a wood stove stands in the kitchen area, don't use it. Someone has disconnected the outflow pipe and a large note claims that it is dangerous to use. But the cabin is still comfortable and a small cook stove should heat portions of the cabin quite nicely. Other comforts include a table and chairs, a loft for sleeping (just like "Little House on the Prairie" days), and a pit toilet is located nearby.

The fish at Muskrat Lake were really jumping the day we visited the area. Brook and rainbow trout inhabit the eight acre lake. At 17 feet deep, the lake is also excellent for swimming. A fun way to explore is via a homemade log raft that floats in a small channel, begging to go out on the lake. The raft comes complete with homemade oars.

To reach Upper Snowshoe Lake continue hiking through the trees, passing large meadows along the way. This is a good place

70

to look for wildflowers during the early summer months. At 6.4 miles come to a junction and see Winopee Lake off to the left. A spur trail leads to the 40 acre lake which is stocked with brook and rainbow trout. At 32 feet deep, it is also perfect for swimming. Hikers will find plenty of campsites around the lake as well.

Turn right at the junction, now following the sign to Upper Snowshoe Lake. Climb gradually to Lower Snowshoe Lake at 6.7 miles. Rocky outcrops stand scattered here and there around the 18 acre lake, a good spot for swimming. You'll find plenty of campsites. Brook trout live in the lake.

Pass tiny three acre Middle Snowshoe Lake (also stocked with brook trout and rainbow trout) on your way to Upper Snowshoe Lake at 7.4 miles. Several campsites are located at the 7.6 miles mark where you'll also find a meadow.

Spanning 30 acres, Upper Snowshoe is the largest of the Snowshoe Lakes, but at eight feet deep it is the shallowest of the three. The lake is stocked with brook trout.

Muskrat Lake cabin

26 MINK LAKE LOOP

Distance: 20.1 miles (complete loop)
Elevation gain: 1,920 feet; loss 1,920 feet
High point: 5,760 feet
Usually open: July through October
Topographic map: The Three Sisters
                 Wilderness Map
Obtain map from: Deschutes National
                 Forest, Willamette
                 National Forest

Lakes are more numerous here, in the Mink Lake Basin area, than in any other portion of the Three Sisters Wilderness. In addition, you'll also find the largest lake in the Wilderness, lovely Mink Lake.

The loop begins at the Six Lakes Trailhead, located 35 miles west of Bend via the Cascades Lakes Highway (Oregon Highway No. 46). A sign "Six Lakes Trailhead" points the way to a large gravel parking area. One pit toilet is provided for your convenience.

Begin hiking Six Lakes Trail No. 14 at a near level grade through lodgepoles pines to 0.9 mile. A spur trail heads off to the right and leads to the northeast side of Blow Lake. Turn left toward Doris Lake and cross a bridge then reach another spur trail leading to Blow Lake at 1.0 mile. Blow Lake is a nice size lake (45 acres) stocked with brook trout.

From here, hike through a forest of lodgepole pine with some western white pine, mountain hemlock, and true fir mixed in. Dwarf huckleberry carpet portions of the ground. The trail to Doris Lake is fairly level or a gradual climb until reaching the lake at 2.2 miles.

A pretty lake, 71 foot deep, 90 acre Doris Lake is good for swimming and fishing brook and rainbow trout. Several good campsites are available and a rocky butte provides a splendid backdrop to the west side of the lake. Please note: several campsites are in the process of being restored to a natural state. Please do not camp in these areas.

Continue up at a gradual rate to a junction at 3.2 miles. The trail to the left leads past Senoj Lake, 0.5 mile distant. Stay to the right and hike toward the Pacific Crest Trail (PCT). Soon after this point, hike across a forested slope to 4.1 miles and a crest which

is also the dividing line between the Willamette and Deschutes National Forests. Now begin a gradual downhill to the PCT junction at 5.1 miles.

The trail heading off to the left to Horseshoe Lake is the return trail for this loop. To the right, the PCT heads to Island Lake and north to Canada. Hike straight ahead to Vera Lake.

Gradually descend to Vera Lake at 5.3 miles. Although the map shows the lake on the right (north) side of the trail, it is actually on the left or south side. While only two acres in size, the lake is stocked with rainbow trout.

Continue past Vera Lake, passing several small meadows along the way and crossing a small stream at 5.6 miles. Near the stream see a spur trail leading down to a large camp and meadow.

It's mostly a gradual down or level to a junction at 7.2 miles. Now big firs stand tall, and bear grass and huckleberries cover the ground. At the junction the sign points the way to Goose Lake located close to the junction. Current maps do not list Goose Lake, but you'll find it marked on the old maps. This trail leads past Goose Lake to Corner Lake, 0.5 mile away.

To continue to Mink Lake, head left to Porky Lake. Pass a small, lilypad-covered lake at 7.6 miles and at 7.7 miles see Porky Lake off to the left. Another 0.2 mile down the trail and you'll see a definite trail leading to a large camp. Rainbow and brook trout inhabit the lake.

Stay level now to a junction at 8.1 miles to Mud Lake. Keep straight and reach the junction to Mink Lake at 8.3 miles. Turn right and moderately climb to 8.8 miles and a junction to an unmaintained trail to Corner Lake.

Continue 200 feet to a fork in the trail. There is a view of Mink Lake from here. As mentioned, Mink Lake is the largest of all the Three Sisters Lakes, and stretches across some 360 acres. Several kinds of trout live in the 70 foot deep lake. These include cutthroat, rainbow, and brook trout.

Head right to continue the loop around the lake and reach the Mink Lake Shelter on the left at 8.9 miles. If the shelter is occupied, you'll find plenty of sites for camping nearby. Please choose a site at least 100 feet from the lake. (As you make the loop around the lake, you'll pass several restoration sites.

The Forest Service asks that you refrain from walking through or camping in these areas.)

The trail around the lake passes through the trees at a nearly level grade. At 9.9 miles find the Junction Lake junction. Stay straight and reach the Elk Creek Trailhead junction at 10.0 miles. Again keep straight ahead, now hiking toward South Lake. As you hike around the lake, you'll get a couple views of South Sister and Broken Top.

Reach another junction at 11.0 miles. Before this point, rhododendrons brighten up the lakeshore during the late spring and early summer months. Now head away from the lake and to the right, climbing moderately, then level across a ridge. Later hike up and down at a moderate grade to the PCT junction at 11.7 miles.

Turn left and continue past an unnamed lake near the junction. Gradually descend through the trees to Mac Lake at 12.1 miles. Rainbow trout and brook trout live in this 70 acre lake. Campsites are few due to the thick vegetation which blankets the ground.

At 12.5 miles pass Merritt Lake, then it's a gradual up and down to Horseshoe Lake at 12.9 miles. Fourteen feet deep and 60 acres, Horseshoe Lake is also stocked with both brook and rainbow trout. A good campsite can be found near the northwest end of the lake.

Head across a forested slope now, gradually climbing to 13.5 miles and a glimpse of Porky Lake. Shortly thereafter, head away from the slope to a junction at 13.7 miles. Porky Lake is a steep descent to the left. Walk about a hundred feet farther to a spur trail to Cliff Lake. The spur leads approximately 100 yards to a shelter and several good areas for camping.

There are rocky cliffs surrounding portions of the 40 acre lake, which is 24 feet deep, good for swimming and stocked with brook trout.

Back on the main trail, continue past a large rock flow, hiking past hemlock draped with gray-green moss. At 15.0 miles meet back up with the Six Lakes Trail, turn right and continue back to the trailhead at 20.1 miles.

Trail in Mink Lake Basin

27 GREEN LAKES TRAILHEAD TO MORAINE LAKE

Distance: 3.3 miles (one-way)
Elevation gain: 1000 feet; loss 50 feet
High point: 6,450 feet
Usually open: July through October
Topographic map: The Three Sisters
Wilderness Map
Obtain map from: Deschutes National
Forest, Willamette
National Forest

Gorgeous, with a spectacular view of South Sister, Moraine Lake is a popular base camp for those climbing the 10,358 foot mountain. Because it is popular, expect to share the lake with someone else, especially on the weekends.

To reach the Green Lakes Trailhead drive west from Bend, via the Cascades Lakes Highway (Oregon Highway No. 46) for 27 miles. A large parking area is located across the road from Sparks Lake. Hikers will find pit toilets for their convenience. Also, a horse ramp is available.

The Green Lakes Trail originates at the northwest end of the parking area. Pass a Forest Service bulletin board and enter the Wilderness in 100 yards. Cross over Fall Creek via a bridge at 0.1 mile. Now begin a gradual climb through a forest of primarily hemlock and some true fir to the Moraine Lake junction at 2.2 miles.

The trail to your right leads to the Green Lakes Basin (see #24 BROKEN TOP/GREEN LAKES LOOP for more information). Turn left and climb the gradual, occasionally moderate trail, passing between a large rock flow at 2.6 miles.

A view of Mount Bachelor is possible at this point, then head back into the trees, later crossing through a semi-open area and eventually out into the open. There's a good view of Broken Top at 2.9 miles. In addition, there's a view of South Sister from Moraine Lake at 3.3 miles. From Moraine Lake, South Sister is not a technical climb. (For more information see #28 MORAINE LAKE TO SOUTH SISTER.)

Moraine Lake is a high mountain lake located at the 6,450 foot level. Several campsites rest around the 12 acre jewel. Stocked with brook trout, anglers will want to throw in their lines. At 23 feet deep, the lake is also popular for swimming.

Moraine Lake

CENTRAL OREGON WILDERNESS AREAS

28 MORAINE LAKE TO SOUTH SISTER

Distance: 3.4 miles (one-way)
Elevation gain: 3,908 feet; loss 0 feet
High point: 10,358 feet
Usually open: August through early
October
Topographic map: The Three Sisters
Wilderness Map
Obtain map from: Deschutes National
Forest, Willamette
National Forest

From atop South Sister, you'll feel as though you can see forever. To the south, Diamond Peak, Mount Thielsen, Mount McLoughlin and countless other peaks and lakes are visible. On a super clear day it's possible to see Mount Shasta, more than a hundred miles away.

To the east/southeast, view Broken Top, Mount Bachelor, Bend, and points farther. And to the north you'll see a variety of alpine lakes, the Middle and North Sisters; Three Fingered Jack; Mt. Jefferson, the state's second highest peak; Mt. Hood, Oregon's highest; and Mt. Adams, located in Washington state. To the west, see more of the Three Sisters Wilderness and the Coast Range.

Several trails lead up to the summit, some rated more difficult than the others. In fact, certain routes require special skills and climbing equipment. We chose the route leading from Moraine Lake. The climb is not technical at all, just a good, long, steep hike up the mountain.

It's possible to climb the mountain in one day. If you opt to climb the summit from the Green Lakes trailhead, you'll climb a total of 4,908 feet in elevation for 6.7 miles. Or, you can hike to Moraine Lake as this guide suggests, and reach the summit from there. (See #27 GREEN LAKES TRAILHEAD TO MORAINE LAKE for directions to Moraine Lake.)

Climbing times to the top of South Sister vary with the individual. Because we spend our summers hiking and biking, we were able to hike from the Green Lakes Trailhead to the top of South Sister in just under five hours.

At Moraine Lake, we met two admirable human beings. One was a 8-year old boy, the other, a 76-year old man, both of whom had made the climb from the lake to the summit the day before. It was the man's fourth time up the mountain, the boy's first. The boy made it to the top in six hours, the man made it in 5.5 hours. Both proved that if you are in good health, and determined to reach the top, you can. Most important of all, take your time, and enjoy.

Before you begin your climb you'll want to be sure to bring plenty of water, food, and warm clothing for it can be cold and windy on the summit. And please, never climb in bad weather or when the weather service predicts a storm. A warm, sunny day can change into blizzard conditions before you'd have time to reach the warmer confines of the forest floor.

From Moraine Lake you'll see several trails leading north across a wide alpine basin. Choose a trail and hike the level grade to 0.4 mile then begin a steep climb out of the basin. Meet up with several other trails once you are out of the basin and heading up the south slope of the mountain.

Beautiful views are possible along the way as you climb the steep grade. Notice the twisted pines and delicate plants found at this elevation. At 2.0 miles reach a crest and the south end of the Lewis Glacier, a massive glacier blanketing the southeast side of the mountain. Also, you'll see a lake just below the crest. In addition, notice the trail leading to the right and down to Green Lakes.

Head left and up the cinder-covered slopes now. As you climb, you may become increasingly annoyed at the loose scree. Think positive, however. You'll be at the summit in no time.

At 3.1 miles reach the south end of the crater rim for a spectacular view of your surroundings. Notice the snow and ice that fills much of the crater and surrounds two small sky-blue lakes. A nearly flat trail leads around the crater rim to the true summit at 3.4 miles.

As you circle the crater you'll see numerous rock shelters that previous climbers have made, many of whom spent the night on the mountain. What a truly unique experience that must be!

Moraine Lake and South Sister

CENTRAL OREGON WILDERNESS AREAS

29 UPPER AND LOWER PROXY FALLS

Distance: 0.6 miles (one-way)
Elevation gain: 50 feet; loss 0 feet
High point: 3,200 feet
Usually open: March through November
Topographic map: The Three Sisters
Wilderness Map
Obtain map from: Deschutes National
Forest, Willamette
National Forest

The Proxy Falls trail is short but sweet. Perfect for those interested in a beautiful little hike and especially for those with children. Like a L.A. freeway, the trail is heavily used on weekends and holidays, but worth a trip during the week when crowds are few. Perhaps the best time to visit is in the early morning when you can have the falls all to yourself.

To reach the falls, travel east on Oregon Hwy. 126 from McKenzie Bridge. You'll find a market in town, a gas station a couple miles to the west. At 4.8 miles reach the junction of Oregon Hwys. 126 and 242. Turn right on Oregon 242, a narrow paved highway closed during the winter months. (The road is usually open sometime in June or July. Check with the Forest Service for opening dates each year.) Travel trailers are not recommended. Trucks, trailers and motor homes more than a combined length of 50 feet are prohibited.

Continue 8.8 miles to the trailhead where you'll find plenty of room to park. Enter the Wilderness via Proxy Falls Trail No. 3532.

Climb gradually, hiking through ancient lava flows where a vast array of wildflowers bloom in the spring. Pines, firs, rhododendrons, and huckleberries decorate most of the trail.

At 0.3 mile reach a junction. Upper Falls is located 0.1 mile to the left. Upper Proxy Falls tumbles down in two distinct cascades, spilling over mossy rocks into a deep pool. Notice that the pool doesn't empty into a nearby stream. It just seems to disappear. We wondered where the water went, but surprisingly the Forest Service has never done any tests. For now it is a mystery!

What they do know is that the unrelated falls, which come from two different water sources, formed when Collier Crater erupted over 600 years ago. During this time, basalt dams blocked Proxy Creek.

The ground is quite porous, due to the recent flow, allowing the water spilling into the pool at the base of Upper Proxy Falls to "disappear."

Head back 0.1 mile to the junction. Head to Lower Falls which you'll see in another 0.1 mile for a total of 0.6 mile for the entire one-way hike.

There's a good view of Lower Proxy Falls from the railing. The 200 foot falls plunge down over mossy green stones, spraying mist outward and skyward, raining upon the surrounding plants 24 hours a day.

Viewing waterfalls such as these provide memories to last a lifetime. So others can experience the same beautiful memories, please remember to pack out all trash, bury all toilet paper, and answer nature's call at least 100 feet from any water source.

Lower Proxy Falls

Linton Lake

30 LINTON LAKE

Distance: 1.2 miles (one-way)
Elevation gain: 150 feet; loss 180 feet
High point: 3,600 feet
Usually open: June through November
Topographic map: The Three Sisters
Wilderness Map
Obtain map from: Deschutes National
Forest, Willamette
National Forest

Linton Lake is a charming lake, perfect for day hiking with the kids, rafting on azure waters, or fishing for a prized trout.

To reach the 75 acre lake, travel east on Oregon Hwy. 126 from McKenzie Bridge. You'll find a market in town, a gas station a couple miles to the west. At 4.8 miles reach the junction of Oregon Hwy. 126 and Oregon Hwy. 242. Turn right on Hwy. 242, a narrow paved highway closed during the winter months. (Check with the Forest Service for opening dates each year. It is usually open sometime in June or July.) Travel trailers are not recommended. Trucks, trailers and motor homes more than a combined length of 50 feet are prohibited.

Reach the Linton Lake Trailhead at 10.3 miles. About 1.5 miles before reaching the trailhead, you'll pass the Proxy Falls Trailhead. (See #29 UPPER AND LOWER PROXY FALLS for more information.)

Enter the Wilderness upon hiking Linton Lake Trail No. 3519. (There's a shortcut to Linton Lake, but parking is limited and located on a blind curve. If you'd prefer using the Linton Lake Cutoff Trail No. 3519A, however, drive another 0.5 mile to the trailhead. It cuts 0.4 mile one-way off your hike.)

Climb gradually to 0.7 mile and the Linton Lake Cutoff Trail junction. Scattered lava fields, and high mountain timber grace the surrounding landscape, while rhododendrons bloom early in the season. An occasional striped snake may scurry through the dry leaves, startling an unwary hiker.

At 0.9 miles begin a moderate downhill, reaching Linton Lake at 1.2 miles. Picnic sites are few at this section of the lake. I suggest hiking the spur trail which leads around a portion of the lake for a better picnic area.

An unmaintained trail encircles the 82 foot deep lake at a fairly level grade with some gradual ups and downs. During the early summer months, portions of the trail are soggy and slippery. Be careful, particularly when stepping across exposed tree roots.

Notice Linton Falls to the east. Soon, you'll lose the view of the falls as you head closer to it, but the sound of water cascading hundreds of feet will only increase in volume.

About 0.4 mile around the lake and you'll see some campsites which are located too close to the lake, but seem to be the only areas available for camping. For a magnificent sight, continue another 0.3 mile or so to Linton Creek.

The creek is an exciting place. Like a washing machine gone haywire, the turbulent waters swirl and plunge, banging against rocks and logs with a thunderous boom. Notice the huge old trees, especially one monster that must be six feet across in several sections that have fallen across the creek. The area is perfect for a picnic. There are a couple more campsites located nearby.

Anglers have the opportunity to hook two kinds of trout, brook and brown, either from the shore or from a raft as some folks do. We picked up empty bait containers while hiking the lake. Please, remember to pack out all garbage!

Viewing pristine areas such as these supply memories to last a lifetime. Remember, however, others want to experience the same beautiful memories. Please, pack out all trash, bury all toilet paper, and respond to nature's call at least 100 feet from any water source.

31 OLALLIE MOUNTAIN

Distance: 3.6 miles (one-way)
Elevation gain: 1,308 feet; loss 80 feet
High point: 5,708 feet
Usually open: June or July through October
Topographic map: The Three Sisters Wilderness Map
Obtain map from: Deschutes National Forest, Willamette National Forest

The view from atop Olallie Mountain is magnificent, and the wildflower display near the summit is truly remarkable if you catch it early in the season.

To reach the trailhead, travel via Oregon Hwy. 126, located four miles east of the small town of Blue River. There's a cafe, ice cream shop, store, and gas station in town.

Turn right on paved FS Road No. 19, crossing by bridge over the crystal-clear McKenzie River, and heading south toward Cougar Reservoir. Reach the reservoir and a junction at 3.3 miles. Head left on FS Road No. 1993, now driving across the dam then turning to the right toward Echo Campground and boat launch area.

Reach the Echo day use area in another 2.5 miles. Make a left at the junction, remaining on FS Road No. 1993 which is now a well-maintained gravel road. Stay on No. 1993 and reach the trailhead in 11.6 miles. There's room to park.

Begin hiking the Olallie Trail through the trees at a gradual rate, passing a wilderness sign at 0.1 mile. Continue, hiking gradual or level to 0.6 mile and a creek. Near the 1.2 miles mark look for Mt. Bachelor through the trees to the east. At 1.8 miles reach another small stream. Both streams usually run all year, but not always.

You'll hike past some large Douglas fir along the scenic route. Hemlock also dot the landscape. Bear grass, ferns, rhododendrons and other vegetation reassures the forest floor. Just before reaching a saddle at 2.2 miles, you'll climb at a moderate pitch, an illustration of things to come. Turn right onto the Olallie Mountain Trail. Olallie Trail descends to Olallie Meadow, Olallie Mountain Trail doesn't go to Olallie Meadow. It leads to the summit.

Now you'll hike through fields of lush foot-tripping bear grass while climbing the steep grade through trees and rich meadows. Huckleberries, vanilla leaf, trilliums, lilies, false hellebore and other colorful species garnish the angled slopes.

At 3.2 miles begin a slight downhill, then it's a steep, winding uphill to Olallie Mountain, 3.6 miles from the trailhead. Numerous wildflowers sway in the gentle breeze or whip from side to side in the brisk winds near and on top of the summit. Look for fragrant Washington lilies, columbine, paintbrush, wild roses, scarlet gilia, and asters to name a few.

You'll find a well-maintained lookout atop the 5,708-foot peak. Open only during the summer months, there's a visitor register begging for your signature inside. It seems as though everyone has only good thoughts to include in the log. There are few complaints. Some whined about the steep grade, others said it was an easy hike for such a magnificent view. Most claim the view is "awesome, magnificent, God's handiwork." Some don't even see the view: often it is obscured by clouds. Still, by what they have written, they seem content.

From atop the lookout you'll see north to Mt. Hood and south to Diamond Peak and many high mountain peaks between. Also, you can gaze down into a variety of drainages, search the heavens for avian creatures and do so from the comfort of the sheltered lookout if the weather is nasty.

The lookout was built in the 1930s, but is no longer manned. Some say the only year-round resident is a raccoon which hides in the attic. In reality, it is but a tiny pack rat.

Olallie Mountain Lookout

32 YANKEE MOUNTAIN

Distance: 5.7 miles (one-way)
Elevation gain: 880 feet; loss 240 feet
High point: 5,360 feet
Usually open: Late June through October
Topographic map: The Three Sisters Wilderness Map
Obtain map from: Deschutes National Forest
Willamette National Forest

The view from atop Yankee Mountain is not mind-boggling. In fact, you'll get a better view atop nearby Olallie Mountain (See #31 OLALLIE MOUNTAIN for more details). There are several pluses to hiking to Yankee Mountain, however. First, the trail is uncrowded. We hiked it on a Saturday during mid-summer and saw one other couple. They were fast asleep on a ridge and never knew we existed. Also, you'll pass through meadow after meadow, where you'll see a wide variety of plant life and good views too.

To reach the trailhead, travel via Oregon Hwy. 126, located four miles east of the small town of Blue River. You'll find a cafe, ice cream shop, store, and gas station in town.

Turn right on paved FS Road No. 19, crossing by bridge over the crystal-clear McKenzie River, and heading south towards Cougar Reservoir. Reach the reservoir and a junction at 3.3 miles. Head left on FS Road No. 1993, now driving across the dam, then turning to the right toward Echo Campground and the boat launch area.

Reach the Echo day use area in another 2.5 miles. Make a left at the junction, remaining on FS Road No. 1993 which is now a well-maintained gravel road. Stay on No. 1993 and reach the Lowder Mountain/Walker Creek trailhead at the junction of FS Road No. 55 in 9.5 miles.

Both the Lowder Mountain and Walker Creek Trails begin as one from the trailhead. Climb a series of switchbacks at a gradual rate, hiking through the trees to the wilderness boundary sign at 0.1 mile. At 0.6 mile the trail is nearly level as you cross the first of many meadows. Photographers and wildflower admirers will see lupine, asters, paintbrush, columbine, delphinium, lilies

and a host of other species. The best time for flowers is late June, early July. Also at this site, look for Olallie Mountain to the southeast, Mt. Bachelor to the east. Farther along look for a portion of Broken Top's craggy peak, also to the east.

From here until you reach Yankee Mountain, you'll cross one meadow after another. Thimbleberries grow profusely along the trail, often covering the trail with boot-tipping vines. The Forest Service had plans to debrush the trail after our trip in July, 1989, so you may find it free of vines. If not, the trail is still easy to follow. The only disadvantage is getting slimed by spittlebugs. Huge wads of spit-like goo cover much of the plant life, sliming all who pass by. (Spittlebug nymphs cover themselves with the frothy mass of bubbles for protection against predators.)

Mammals, especially bears, pass by regularly when the thimbleberries are ripe. A variety of birds eat the berries as well. Some humans claim the berries have an unpleasant taste, similar to cotton.

Small oases of hemlock and Douglas fir trees, including several huge Doug-fir, usually separate the knee-to-waist high meadows, providing much needed shade on a hot day.

After crossing a large meadow at 1.0 mile, begin a gradual down to a ridge then back up to 1.5 miles and a spur trail. Head to the right for a good view to the north of Mt. Hood on a clear day. Mt. Washington, North and Middle Sister are visible as well.

Back on the trail, look for Diamond Peak to the south. Head down at a gradual pace at 1.8 miles where you'll reach a spring. This spring usually runs about 90% of the year. Reach the junction to the Walker Creek Trail at 2.0 miles. As odd as it may seem, the Walker Creek Trail leads to Lowder Mountain. Stay to the left, via Lowder Mountain Trail, to reach Yankee Mountain.

Over the next few miles you'll descend and then climb again, most of the time hiking at a level or gradual grade. Hike through a meadow where little more than tall ferns grow at 4.5 miles. Climb at a moderate grade however, before reaching a ridge at 5.4 miles.

At this point you'll want to begin climbing Yankee Mountain. You're at the right spot if you see nothing but clear cuts to the west.

Also, you'll begin descending to the northwest if you pass the ridge, reaching a small year-round spring at 5.5 miles. If you go this far, you've missed the easiest route up to the top of Yankee Mountain.

Back at the ridge, begin scrambling up the steep slope and reach the top which is 160 feet higher than the trail. (If you obtain a Three Sisters Wilderness Map, please note that the trail around Yankee Mountain shows it going around the north side of the mountain, not the south side which is the correct side.) If you walk around the summit, you'll have a good view toward the Middle and North Sister. Mt. Jefferson is visible as well. To the south you'll see Diamond Peak.

You can return to the trailhead the same way you hiked in, or if you have the opportunity for a shuttle you can continue along Lowder Mountain Trail for another 5.3 miles, descending to FS Road No. 500, located to the east of Cougar Reservoir.

Lowder Mountain Trail

Llama train crossing Obsidian Creek

CENTRAL OREGON WILDERNESS AREAS

33 FROG CAMP/ OBSIDIAN FALLS/ SCOTT TRAIL LOOP

Distance: 16.5 miles (round-trip)
Elevation gain: 2,400 feet; loss 2,400 feet
High point: 6,800 feet
Usually open: July through October
Topographic map: The Three Sisters
Wilderness Map
Obtain map from: Deschutes National
Forest, Willamette
National Forest

Sometimes in life, we have to take the bitter with the sweet. Such is the case when hiking the following loop. First, the bitter: The heavily used trail from Frog Camp to Obsidian Falls leaves little room for a true wilderness experience. The sweet: Alpine meadows painted with precious wildflowers, great views, lovely Obsidian Falls. But if greeting hiker after hiker during the day or over a period of several days gets you down, you're nearly guaranteed peace and quiet if you hike out via the Scott Trail.

To reach the trailhead drive east from McKenzie Bridge, a small one market, one gas station, one restaurant and one motel town, on Oregon Hwy. 126. At 4.8 miles reach the junction of Oregon Hwys. 126 and 242. Turn right on Oregon 242, a narrow paved highway closed during the winter months. Travel trailers are not recommended. Trucks, trailers and motorhomes more than a combined length of 50 feet are prohibited.

Climb the windy road, traveling 15.3 miles to FS Road No. 250, turnoff for the Obsidian Trailhead. Drive the gravel road for 0.3 mile to the trailhead. (Facilities include an outhouse.) There are separate parking areas for stock vehicles and passenger cars. Parking spots seem to be in abundance, but this area gets extremely crowded. Overflow parking is located at Scott Trail, 0.6 mile farther east on Hwy. 242. The following loop ends via the Scott Trail, however you could hike the loop in reverse if you are so inclined.

Begin hiking Obsidian Trail No. 3528, traveling through the trees, reaching a junction in just 200 feet. Head left to the Scott Trail if you'd like to hike the loop in reverse.

Keep to the right to White Branch Creek to begin the loop.

Lodgepole pine and hemlock decorate the slopes as you climb gradually, and bear grass grows throughout the area. Huckleberries are seen, but not in any great numbers. At 0.6 mile reach the wilderness boundary sign.

Continue to 0.8 mile and a junction to Spring Lake Trail No. 3528B. The trail leads to the southwest 0.5 mile to the three acre lake. Native brook trout inhabit the lake, but there are no reports on whether the fishing is good or not. Several campsites exist.

Keep straight, staying at a gradual, sometimes moderate grade, to a lava flow at 2.9 miles. Enter the flow, now hiking up and down at a gradual rate. Notice the view upon reaching the 3.0 miles mark. You'll see Black Crater, Little Brother, North and Middle Sister, Belknap Crater, Little Belknap and Mt. Washington.

Cross White Branch Creek, a popular camping spot, at 3.5 miles. Notice the sign stating that campfires are prohibited within one-half mile of the trail for the next 2.5 miles. There is no camping within 100 feet of the trail, or water.

The trail forks at the creek. Head left to shorten the loop by traveling Glacier Way Trail No. 3528A. The 0.8 mile trail leads to the PCT, but you'll miss Obsidian Falls and more. Head right to complete the loop.

Climb at a moderate, occasionally steep grade to a meadow at 4.0 miles. Cross the flowery meadow, complete with a good view of both the North and Middle Sister. Travel up and down but mostly up next, until reaching the 4.9 miles mark. Look to the right for the Richard Ward Montague Memorial. Montague lived from 1862 to 1935. The inscription reads, "I will lift up mine eyes to the hills from whence cometh my help." The plaque was erected by the Obsidian Club, from which Montague belonged.

There's a view of South Sister as you leave the memorial, continuing southeast, through some trees but mostly across alpine meadow. Also, you'll encounter a steep upgrade, but then the trail is fairly level to 5.2 miles and the PCT junction. At the PCT, you'll see the Husband to the south and you'll enjoy a good close-up view of all three Sisters, although the South Sister isn't as prominent. Head right to Linton Meadows, left to Obsidian

Falls and the remainder of this loop.

Moderately climb now, heading back into the trees for a short while, and reach Obsidian Falls at 5.5 miles. There's a good view of the falls with an unnecessary trail leading to them. Continue a short distance and you'll reach a point near the top of the falls.

This area is in the process of restoration. Camping is not allowed. However, there are several good sites atop the ridge to the west. The view is outstanding as well. You'll see the Husband and the three Sisters.

It's an easy ford across Obsidian Creek. Now hike level or gradually up and down, passing Sisters Spring and several ponds along the way. Farther along, at the 6.1 miles mark, you'll get a close-up view of Little Brother from the Scott Camp overlook. Scott Camp is a popular camp for climbers intent on scaling North or Middle Sister. North Sister is a technical climb, Middle Sister is a steep walk up, but not as easy as South Sister. An ice axe is recommended most of the year.

Just north of here you'll see Mt. Washington and Three Fingered Jack. Look for a cave on the left at the 6.3 miles mark. Also, just past the cave you'll get a wonderful view of Mt. Jefferson. Moderately descend now, entering Sunshine Meadows and a junction at 6.7 miles. As usual, the views are outstanding.

Glacier Way Trail No. 3528A heads to the left and back 0.8 mile to White Branch Creek. The unmaintained trail to the right is a climbers trail leading to Scott Camp. Keep straight on the PCT, crossing a creek, then gradually dropping through the trees and out of the campground and fire restriction zone at 7.2 miles.

Now the trail is a series of gradual ups and down, passing several meadows along the way. At 7.8 miles you'll reach the south edge of an extensive lava flow. Begin a moderate uphill while viewing Collier Cone in the distance. At 8.4 miles begin hiking the Oppie Dildock Pass (named for an early explorer), a rough lava trail leading 0.6 mile to the top of a box canyon. Switchbacks leading up to the canyon are moderate, but may seem steep because of the loose lava.

Hike at a gradual grade to a variety of other trails leading to several high points along the rim. Turn west, following the main trail to the north rim at 9.2 miles.

Now begin descending at a moderate grade. On a clear day it's possible to see Mt. Hood in the distance. Switchback down the lava slope, later descending at a moderate rate to Minnie Scott Springs at 9.8 miles. Ford the small creek (camp sites nearby) and enter the forest for a short time, then pass a meadow and overtake a ridge at 10.2 miles.

Descend across a cinder slope, crossing another creek at 10.5 miles. Enter a meadow, hiking a level grade to the junction of Scott Trail at 10.7 miles.

Head left, hiking across the meadow (trail isn't visible), but aiming for a rock cairn located on another cinder slope. Moderately climb the slope, then begin a downgrade at 10.9 miles.

Hike in the trees again, descending at a moderate, occasionally steep grade. Enter an open cinder field at 11.4 miles. Along the way there are good views of the three Sisters and Mt. Jefferson. The trail heads across open lava much of the time but stays in the trees as well. Mostly, it follows the north edge of another giant lava flow. There are many potential campsites.

Head back into the trees at 13.1 miles. Now begin a series of gradual ups and downs, mostly descending, however, to a meadow at 15.6 miles. The trail passes to the south of the meadow. Bear grass and huckleberries reappear as you walk through the trees. Notice the old trail which dropped at a very steep grade to the trailhead. The new trail was built in 1988.

At 15.9 miles reach the Frog Camp Trail leading to the south. Hike this nearly level trail, reaching the stock trail at 16.4 miles. Two hundred feet farther and you'll find the people trail. Head right, returning to the trailhead at 16.5 miles.

Middle and North Sister from South Sister

34 BLACK CRATER

Distance: 4.0 miles (one-way)
Elevation gain: 2,372 feet; loss 30 feet
High point: 7,251 feet
Usually open: July through October
Topographic map: The Three Sisters
　　　　　　　　Wilderness Map
Obtain map from: Deschutes National
　　　　　　　　Forest, Willamette
　　　　　　　　National Forest

Stunted pines, steep lava slopes and excellent views should thrill all who make the climb to Black Crater's 7,251 foot summit. The trailhead is easy to reach via Oregon Hwy. 242. From Sisters, a town with all the amenities, travel west on Hwy. 242, driving 11.8 miles to the Black Crater trailhead, located just prior to Windy Point. There's room to park and a sign on the south side of the road.

(Oregon Hwy. 242 is closed during the winter months. Check with the Forest Service for opening dates each year. It usually opens sometime in June or July. Travel trailers are not recommended on the narrow windy paved road. Trucks, trailers and motor homes with a combined length of 50 feet or more are prohibited.)

Begin hiking through the trees, climbing at a steep grade for 0.1 mile. The grade lessens to a moderate ascent now, reaching the wilderness boundary sign at 0.2 mile.

The grade remains moderate for most of the hike although there are steep sections as well. At 1.9 miles see Mt. Hood, Three Fingered Jack, Mt. Jefferson and Mt. Washington through the trees. At 2.0 miles the trail gives each hiker some reprieve with a short downhill and some level or gradual up and down terrain to negotiate.

The break is short-lived, however. Begin a moderate to steep uphill at 2.5 miles, reaching a meadowy slope at 3.0 miles. Lupine and various other species decorate the mountainside. Now you'll head up to the summit, traveling mostly in the open, with some shady trees on occasion.

Reach the summit at 4.0 miles. From the old lookout you'll see south to North and South Sister, Broken Top, and Mt. Bachelor. In addition to extensive lava fields to the north, you'll also see Mt. Washington, Three

Fingered Jack, Mt. Jefferson and Mt. Hood. See the town of Sisters and the mountains and high desert beyond when looking east. Look down 700 feet to the north for a view into the actual crater.

On top of Black Crater

35 CAMP LAKE

Distance: 6.9 miles (one-way)
Elevation gain: 1,859 feet; loss 200 feet
High point: 6,960 feet
Usually open: August through October
Topographic map: The Three Sisters
Wilderness Map
Obtain map from: Deschutes National
Forest, Willamette
National Forest

Camp Lake, one of a series of five Chambers Lakes, is heavily used. It is a popular base camp for those scaling the three Sisters. Those longing for a true wilderness experience should camp elsewhere.

Still, Camp Lake is an awesome place to see, if only for a little while. If you'd like some solitude, and you'd like to visit the lake as well, why not camp some place within a mile or two of the lake and day hike to the lake itself? Or, this trip can make for a nice long day hike.

The trailhead is easy to reach. From Sisters, a quaint little town favored by tourists, travel west on Oregon Hwy. 242, via the McKenzie Pass Scenic Route.

(Hwy. 242 is closed during the winter months. Check each year with the Forest Service for opening dates. It normally opens sometime in June or July. Travel trailers are not recommended on the narrow windy paved road. Trucks, trailers and motor homes with a combined length of 50 feet or more are prohibited.)

Pass an expansive llama farm before reaching FS Road No. 15 at 1.4 miles. Turn left, now driving toward the Pole Creek Trailhead. After 7.1 miles, you'll reach a junction. Keep left on Road No. 15 (The map states this is Road No. 1524), driving another 3.5 miles to the trailhead. You'll find plenty of parking and a pit toilet for your convenience.

Begin a gradual to moderate climb through a forest of primarily lodgepole pine, hemlock and an occasional ponderosa pine, to 0.4 mile and a wilderness boundary sign. Continue to 0.6 mile and a view through the trees of North Sister, Mt. Jefferson and Black Crater.

Reach a junction at 1.4 miles. The trail leading to the right meets the PCT near South Mattheu Lake. Keep straight, now hiking toward Green Lakes.

Descend gradually, then moderately, to Soap Creek at 2.0 miles. There are many campsites in the area, most too close to the water. Cross the creek via a log bridge.

(Special Note: You'll cross three creeks before reaching Camp Lake. All three usually flow all summer.)

There's a trail junction just across the creek. The trail heading to the left continues to Green Lakes. Stay straight, now hiking to Chambers Lakes which also leads to Camp Lake.

Climb at a gradual to moderate grade to 2.7 miles and a dry creek. Continue, sometimes via switchbacks across a semi-open slope, although they are not shown on the map. Reach a sparkling little creek at 4.0 miles. Purple lupine and red paintbrush line the creek.

Remain mostly in the trees, hiking past an occasional lupine speckled meadow. It's a gradual climb to North Fork Squaw Creek at 4.6 miles. Notice the campsite just prior to this point.

Ford the creek (easiest later in the summer) or cross via several fallen trees. A sign marks a trail junction on the opposite side of the creek. Walk past the sign then immediately switchback up toward Camp Lake. Another trail leads straight to Demaris Lake, 0.8 mile away. Demaris Lake, a pretty lake with several good campsites, is usually not too crowded.

Climb moderately, traveling much of the time in the open now, to 4.8 miles and a view of eastern Oregon. Before this point, see Middle and North Sister through the trees. There are far better views up ahead.

At 5.0 miles encounter the steepest grade of the entire climb. It is a short climb, though, then levels off somewhat. Hike in and out of the trees, to a wonderful view of South Sister. Descend gradually at 5.2 miles then immediately begin a moderate uphill climb past a tarn and up a ridge. At 5.6 miles hike across a level cinder plain. From here you'll get a good look at both Diller and Hayden glaciers. Also, notice all the stunted whitebark pine, hemlock and fir trees.

At 5.8 miles begin a gradual climb again, through open rocky terrain. Some hardy flowers decorate the slopes, as do gnarly trees. At 6.7 miles begin a gradual downhill to Camp Lake at 6.9 miles.

From the seven acre lake there is an excellent view of South Sister. Walk to the south end of the lake for a good view of Middle and North Sister as well.

Camp Lake is a popular base camp for those climbing all three summits, although Middle Sister is certainly the most popular choice from this spot. Also, many choose to explore the other four Chambers Lakes from Camp Lake and some hike across the saddle between the South and Middle Sister, crossing to the west slope and the PCT.

There are several camp sites at the other Chambers Lake. Firewood is nonexistent however: please pack in a stove if you want a hot meal.

(Special Note: "A Carver Lake Hazard Alert" has been issued by the Deschutes National Forest. Located on the northeast flank of the South Sister, Carver Lake may pose a threat to recreationists in the area. Researchers believe that the natural dam holding the lake could fail, causing flooding down Squaw Creek and on into the town of Sisters. Contact the Forest Service for more information.)

Camp Lake and South Sister

INTRODUCTION TO THE WALDO LAKE WILDERNESS

Numerous small lakes dot the land, sparkling like exquisite gems, shimmering in the sunlight. Pink rhododendrons bloom from mid-June through mid-July, brightening up many of the trails that lead across the vast forest. And throughout the Waldo Lake Wilderness, old-growth pines and firs stand tall, reaching for the heavens.

Located about 20 miles east of Oakridge, the Waldo Lake Wilderness rests on the western slope of the Oregon Cascades, in the Western Cascades and High Cascades province. Steep, dissected slopes are typical of the Western Cascades. Moderate slopes and many lakes, meadows, and rock outcrops are symbolic of the High Cascades.

The preserve ranges in elevation from a low of 2,800 feet along the North Fork Willamette River to a high of 7,144 feet atop Fuji Mountain, a summit providing wonderful views into the entire area and points farther in the distance.

The concept for a Waldo Lake Wilderness began before 1970 with the North Waldo Study Plan. Years later, with the signing of the Oregon Wilderness Bill on June 26, 1984, the 37,162 acre Wilderness was established. Administered under the 1964 Wilderness Act, the basis for all wilderness management, the preserve is managed to uphold "the wilderness character of the land."

The Oakridge Ranger District of the Willamette National Forest has control over the area. You'll find their office in Westfir, several miles west of the town of Oakridge.

Named for Waldo Lake, one of the world's purest lakes, located just outside the eastern Wilderness boundary, the area sits near the crest of the Cascade Mountains. Sitting up high, at the 5,414 foot elevation mark, Oregon's second largest lake (the Upper Klamath/ Agency Lake complex is larger) spans more than 10 square miles and has nearly 22 miles of shoreline. Also Oregon's second deepest lake (at 1932 feet, Crater Lake is the deepest) Waldo Lake reaches to a maximum depth of 420 feet.

According to geologists, the indigo blue waters of Waldo are pure (it's possible to see to depths of 100 feet on a calm day) because the lake has no established inlets to send nutrients into the lake for plant growth. As a result, only two forms of moss exist. Thus, a lack of plant life contributes to Waldo's purity.

Glacial activity has done much to shape the Waldo Lake Basin and surrounding areas. Researchers believe that about 12,000 years ago the area was the center of a large glacial cap, nearly 15,000 feet thick. Eventually the glacier melted, scraping and scooping out more than 800 lakes and potholes, including Waldo Lake which sits in a large glacial depression. As you hike through the area look for the u-shaped troughs, moraine deposits, countless potholes, and other glacial evidence visible today.

A trail leads 21.8 miles around the lake itself, passing many sandy beaches along the way. The beaches are a result of the eruption of Mt. Mazama, a caldera which now holds Crater Lake. About 6,600 years ago the mountain erupted, depositing a two foot thick blanket of pumice over the Waldo area. According to researchers, "it was the silicates in this pumice that formed Waldo Lake's beautiful sandy beaches."

Visitors have used Waldo's beaches for years now with the site becoming popular back in the late 1800's. In fact, the area was supposedly a "major attraction."

Today, 84 miles of trails penetrate the Wilderness, all maintained in a primitive state by the Forest Service. A Forest Service report states, "Hikers and packers can expect some step-over logs, stream crossings without bridges, and brush across trails."

Hikers will find campgrounds on the east side of Waldo Lake. Boats can cruise the lake at 10 mph speed limit which helps to keep the noise level down. While mountain bikes are not allowed in any designated wilderness area, bikers may ride the trail that surrounds the lake.

The wilderness boundary is just west of the lake's west side. Hikers on the west side will not see east side campgrounds. Protecting the alpine atmosphere was a top consideration when campground construction took place, thus east side camps are not visible from the west side of the lake.

In addition to the countless lakes found here, there are many small streams flowing throughout the Wilderness. Most eventually make their way to the larger tributaries of the North Fork of the Willamette River. The fishing is good in many of the streams and rivers with the best fishing found at the Wilderness lakes. The Oregon Department of Fish and Wildlife stocks the lakes on a regular basis. Fishing licenses are required.

State of Oregon game laws apply to hunters utilizing the Wilderness as well. A high mountain deer season for bucks is usually held for one week in September, and the regular deer season extends for an average of three weeks in October. The elk season runs for about two weeks in November. Check with the Oregon State Fish and Wildlife Commission for a complete list of regulations.

Wildlife is abundant in the area although most people do not see much of it. But there is always a thrill in just knowing they are there. Roosevelt elk, black-tailed deer and black bear are common throughout the area. Mule deer inhabit the east side of the Cascades, but intermingle with the black-tails near the crest of the Cascades. Seen on a rare occasion, elusive cougar live in the area as well.

Deer and elk move out of the area to lower elevations as the onslaught of fall snows begin. Mule deer migrate in an easterly direction into central Oregon. The black-tailed deer and Roosevelt elk move westward toward the North Fork of the Willamette River and the Salmon Creek drainage.

Many small mammals inhabit the Wilderness. These include squirrels, mink, marten, weasel, raccoon, bobcat, and coyote. A variety of bird life is also in evidence with species such as the bald eagle and osprey seen near some of the lakes. Also, there are the usual jays, a variety of owls, and game birds such as blue and ruffed grouse.

An unwelcome form of insect life, the mosquito, is abundant from July through the first half of August. Hikers should use mosquito repellant. When the season is at its peak you may want to use a mosquito net as well.

The Wilderness is a popular place during the latter part of summer when the mosquitoes are all but gone. Most people come to camp, hike, hunt, fish, swim, picnic, or just sightsee. Heavy snowfall attracts winter visitors with many of the trails used by cross-country skiers.

Indeed, the Waldo Lake Wilderness is a popular place today, but researchers believe the Waldo Lake area has been "popular" for thousand of years. Stone tool artifacts found scattered throughout the area indicate "that Native Americans inhabited the area thousands of years before white settlers arrived."

White settlers of the late 1800's and early 1900's found the Waldo area highly suitable for sheep grazing. During the same time, trappers also used the area to trap fur-bearing animals. In fact, South Waldo Lake was the location of many winter encampments for trappers from the Oakridge and La Pine areas.

Waldo Lake was named for Judge John Breckenridge Waldo, who explored much of the Cascade region and originated the idea of creating the Cascade Range Forest Reserve. Designation of the reserve finally came on September 27, 1893.

Long before the white man arrived, however, ancient western red cedars took hold, growing along the North Fork Willamette River. Today, some of the 800 year old giants stand alongside the Shale Ridge Trail. (See #40 SHALE RIDGE TRAIL for more information.)

Man has found many uses for the cedar tree. Modern man uses red cedar as the chief wood for shingles. Also, it is used for siding, fenceposts, utility poles, and boatbuilding. In previous years, Northwest Coast Indians carved totem poles and split lumber for their lodges using this durable, rot-resistant softwood. Also known as "Canoe-cedar," the trees were named after the special war canoes hollowed out of massive cedar trunks by the Indians. In addition, the Indians fashioned boxes, batons, helmets, roof thatching, blankets, and cloaks from the wood or fibrous inner bark.

A visit to the Waldo Lake Wilderness can provide a lesson in history, the chance to view wildlife or swim in pure water.

For more information contact the following: Oakridge Ranger District
46375 Highway 58
Westfir, OR. 97492
(503) 782-2291

View from Fuji Mountain toward Diamond Peak

36 ROAD NO. 5883 TO FUJI MOUNTAIN

Distance: 1.5 miles (one-way)
Elevation gain: 944 feet; loss 0 feet
High point: 7,144 feet
Usually open: July through October
Topographic map: The Waldo Lake Area
                Map
Obtain map from: Willamette National
                Forest

Spectacular views are possible from atop windy Fuji Mountain, the highest point in the Waldo Lake Wilderness. There is plenty of shade for those hiking the trail up to the summit on a hot summer day.

There are two entry points to the Fuji Mountain Trail; a long trail and a short trail. The long trail begins off Waldo Lake Road and leads 5.6 miles to the summit. The short route begins off FS Road No. 5883 and leads 1.5 miles to the same great view.

The following guide describes the short route, a hike perfect for children, or those in the mood for a relatively easy stroll.

To reach the trailhead drive to Eagle Creek Road (FS Road No. 5883), located 15.3 miles southeast of Oakridge. Head north on No. 5883, driving until you reach the trailhead at 10.7 miles.

Begin hiking Fuji Mountain Trail No. 3674 at the sign. The trail leads up through a logged area, then into the trees until reaching the summit. At 0.2 mile reach a junction which heads right to the South Waldo Shelter, left to the top of Fuji Mountain.

Lupines and several other flower species brighten up the trail as it climbs moderately to 1.2 miles and a rock outcrop where there is a nice view. Continue across the slope then up a ridge to the top of Fuji Mountain at 1.5 miles.

The view from atop the mountain is quite impressive. All of the Waldo Mountain Wilderness stretches out before those who make the climb. To the east, Waldo Lake, one of the purest lakes in the world, borders the preserve. To the north, hikers will see several Cascade giants. These include Mount Bachelor, Broken Top, the three Sisters, Mount Washington, Mount Jefferson, and Mount Hood. To the east, see Maiden Peak, Twin Peaks, Mount Ray, and Odell Lake. To the south, view both the Diamond Peak and Mount Thielsen Wilderness Areas.

At one time a fire lookout stood atop Fuji Mountain. Established in 1925, the lookout began as an open platform with a firefinder. The person manning the lookout lived in a tent. In 1928, a cupola-type structure replaced the open platform and in 1959 a cabin-type structure replaced the cupola. The Forest Service removed the lookout in 1968.

It is believed that the lookout was manned up until that time: a fire lookout stood guard only during heavy lightning activity. Fire patrol by aircraft replaced many of the old manned lookouts in Oregon. Fire patrols continue today with two flights daily during the summer months.

37 GANDER LAKE/ SWAN LAKE TRAIL

Distance: 2.0 miles (one-way)
Elevation gain: 1,000 feet; loss 100 feet
High point: 5,300 feet
Usually open: June through October
Topographic map: The Waldo Lake Area Map
Obtain map from: Willamette National Forest

Lush vegetation, plenty of blooming rhododendrons early in the season, and the beauty of Gander and Swan Lakes make this steep trail well worth the effort.

To reach the trailhead drive from downtown Oakridge, turning north off Oregon Highway 58 at the only stop light. Turn right shortly thereafter, following the sign to Salmon Creek Road No. 24.

Pass Salmon Creek Falls, a nice place for swimming, taking pictures, a picnic, or camping before reaching the junction to FS Road No. 2417 at 11.3 miles. Head left on No. 2417, driving another 5.8 miles before the road turns to well-maintained gravel. Stay straight and continue another 3.0 miles to an unsigned road. The trailhead lies at the end of this unsigned road, 0.8 mile ahead.

Gander Lake Trail No. 3568 is not signed as such, but there is a sign pointing the way to an unnamed trail. Begin hiking in the open, then enter old-growth forest.

The trail leads across a couple of ups and downs, then up at a moderate to steep grade. Lush vegetation blankets much of the forest with ferns and rhododendrons in abundance.

At 1.1 miles the trail flattens off somewhat and leads past a pond on the right. Reach a junction at 1.3 miles. Head to the right for the Waldo Meadows Trail.

Gander Lake is visible just up ahead. A spur trail leads directly to the 32 foot deep lake, bordered by thick rhododendrons. The rhody's usually bloom in mid-June to mid-July. Anglers will find good fishing for both brook and rainbow trout. Few campsites exist around the 58-acre lake.

To continue to Swan Lake, head back to the junction and up the trail climbing moderate to steep once again. Reach a spur trail to Swan Lake at 2.0 miles. (You'll find the spur trail to the right of a sign off the main trail, pointing the way back to Gander Lake.) Swan Lake is 100 yards from the main trail.

Swan Lake is a pretty lake with views of Waldo Mountain and plenty of rhododendrons. There are very few potential campsites around the 10-acre lake. Fishermen will find the lake stocked with brook and cutthroat trout.

Swan Lake

38 WALDO MOUNTAIN/ SALMON LAKES LOOP

Distance: 8.9 miles (complete loop)
Elevation gain: 1,957 feet; loss 1,957 feet
High point: 6,357 feet
Usually open: July through October
Topographic map: The Waldo Lake Area
Map
Obtain map from: Willamette National
Forest

Terrific views of the Waldo Lake Wilderness and many Cascade Peaks are possible on this loop. In addition, early season hikers will see an abundance of rhododendrons, an occasional Washington lily, and other species as well. Anglers will find excellent fishing at the two Salmon Lakes. And at Lake Chetlo hikers will discover a superb lake for swimming.

To reach the trailhead drive from downtown Oakridge, turning north off Oregon Highway 58 at the town's only stop light. Turn right shortly thereafter, following the sign to Salmon Creek Road No. 24.

Pass scenic Salmon Creek Falls, a nice place to swim, picnic, camp, and take pictures, before reaching the junction to FS Road No. 2417 at 11.3 miles. Head left on No. 2417, driving another 5.8 miles before the road turns to well-maintained gravel. Stay straight and continue another 0.4 mile to FS Road No. 2424. Turn right on No. 2424 and reach the trailhead in 3.8 miles.

This loop begins on Salmon Lakes Trail No. 3585. Reach the wilderness boundary and a registration box in 200 feet. (A wilderness permit is not mandatory, but filling out registration cards may help the Forest Service when making future decisions regarding the area.)

Walk another 100 feet to a fork in the trail. Head left, hiking Waldo Mountain Trail No. 3592 through dense forest and lush vegetation which includes bear grass, rhododendrons and Washington lilies. The best time to see the rhododendrons in bloom is between mid-June and mid-July.

It's a steep climb to 0.5 mile. Then it's a moderate up with occasional steep sections to 1.3 miles and an old wilderness boundary

sign. At 2.1 miles reach a junction. Waldo Meadows Trail heads to the right; head left to continue the Waldo Mountain Trail, then curve to the right in 100 feet.

Climb the moderate to steep slope, hiking a ridge to the top of Waldo Mountain and a lookout at 3.1 miles. A volunteer lives in the lookout from July 1 to September 1 each year. Volunteers keep watch for the threat of fire. From the lookout, there is a grand view of several Cascade Peaks to the north. These include Mount Hood, Mount Jefferson, the three Sisters, and many others. Also, gaze down upon the Waldo Lake Wilderness with grand views of Gander and Swan Lakes. Also, see the two Eddeeleo lakes, and the Salmon Lakes as well. Of course, you'll also see Waldo Lake and Diamond Peak. On a clear day see Mary's Peak, the highest mountain in the Coast Range.

Head across the rocky ridge then begin a moderate, sometimes steep descent to the junction of Winchester Ridge Trail No. 3596 at 4.0 miles. Stay straight, heading through old-growth forest now to a junction at 4.5 miles.

The loop continues to the right at this point. Those interested in a nice place to picnic or camp, may want to head left for 0.2 mile and an easy hike to Lake Chetlo. An excellent lake for swimming, the 19-acre lake is listed as a poor fishing lake. You may want to try your luck, however, as brook trout do inhabit the lake.

Back at the junction, turn right on Wahanna Trail No. 3583 and head up then down to another junction at 4.7 miles. Waldo Lake is located down the trail to your left. Continue to Waldo Meadows via Salmon Lakes Trail No. 3585.

It's an easy down to Waldo Meadow which extends from about the 6.0 miles mark and stretches for over one-quarter mile. Look for frogs, crimson columbine, lilies, yarrow, paintbrush, hellebore, ferns, and other colorful flowers.

At 6.4 miles reach a junction to Cupit Mary Trail No. 3559. (Map shows this as the Waldo Meadows Trail No. 3591.) Upper Salmon Lake is an easy 0.4 mile south via this trail. At Upper Salmon Lake there is a good campsite with Waldo Mountain creating a nice backdrop to the 10-acre lake. Lower Salmon Lake can be reached by bushwhacking 0.4 mile to the west of Upper Salmon Lake. Anglers will find good wild brook trout fishing at both lakes.

At the Salmon Lakes/Cupit Mary junction, you'll find an old camp with a large holding pen for stock. The Forest Service plans to tear down the camp soon so it may or may not be there when you visit. Spring water is located to the left of the signed junction and down 200 yards along the well-worn trail.

From the camp reach the junction to Waldo Meadows Trail which leads to the north. Head straight, descending most of the time and pass another old wilderness boundary sign at 7.6 miles.

The trail leads across a steep ridge, but there is plenty of shade for hot, sunny days. At 8.8 miles the trail levels off and heads back into old-growth forest. Reach the Waldo Mountain/Salmon Lakes junction at 8.9 miles. Turn left and head back to the trailhead in 300 feet.

Waldo Mountain Lookout

39 BLACK CREEK TRAIL TO KLOVDAHL BAY

Distance: 3.8 miles (one-way)
Elevation gain: 2,150 feet; loss 50 feet
High point: 5,500 feet
Usually open: June through October
Topographic map: The Waldo Lake Area
                        Map
Obtain map from: Willamette National
                           Forest

Hikers will enjoy dense old-growth, numerous streams, and the roar of Lillian Falls, all before reaching Klovdahl Bay, located on the west side of Waldo Lake. Here, you'll see some of the clearest water in the world as you swim, fish, or sit and enjoy the view.

To reach the trailhead drive from downtown Oakridge, turning north off Oregon Highway 58 at the town's only stop light. Turn right shortly thereafter, following the sign to Salmon Creek Road No. 24.

Pass Salmon Creek Falls, a scenic place for swimming, picnicking, camping, and picture taking, before reaching the junction to FS Road No. 2417 at 11.3 miles. Keep to the right, staying on paved FS Road No. 24 and reach a fork at 3.0 miles.

Head to the left via FS Road No. 2421 (pavement turns to well-maintained gravel 0.4 mile after junction) driving to the Black Creek Trailhead and end of road at 8.8 miles.

Berry bushes are in abundance as you begin hiking Black Creek Trail No. 3551. At 0.1 mile cross a bridge over Edith Creek. Also, enter the wilderness and sign in at the registration box. Wilderness permits are not necessary, but may help the Forest Service in future management of the area.

Climb at a moderate grade, passing through dense old-growth forest of Douglas fir, western red cedar, and mountain hemlock. Delicate maiden hair ferns border some of the streams. At 0.5 mile cross a stream and several other small streams before reaching Lillian Falls at 1.2 miles.

Lillian Falls is a beautiful falls located on Nettie Creek, and is a terrific place for a break. Is there ever enough time to spend watching the waterfalls?

From Lillian Falls, continue up to 1.5 miles, then switchback up and level off some at 1.8 miles. Rhododendrons line some of the trail now, with bear grass also in abundance.

Climb gradually to Nettie Creek at 2.2 miles. Ford the creek and continue up to 2.6 miles, hiking an open slope for a short distance. See Fuji Mountain to the south.

At 2.7 miles ford Klovdahl Creek, then zigzag up to 3.0 miles and flatten off once again. Next, there is a steep grade up then a gradual down to Waldo Lake at 3.8 miles.

From Klovdahl Bay see the Twins to the east, Charlton Butte to the northeast, and the tip of Maiden Peak to the southeast. If you'd like a view of Waldo Lake with South Sister in the background, walk south about 0.5 mile on the Waldo Lake Trail.

Also, about 0.5 mile south via the Waldo Lake Trail, you'll see a spur trail leading off towards the lake and back to the north to the Klovdahl Headgate.

In 1908, the Waldo Lake Irrigation and Power Company was formed, with the intention of providing irrigation water and power to the entire Willamette Valley. As project supervisor, Simon Klovdahl, a Norwegian-born civil engineer based in Eugene, designed the headgates and developed plans for the entire project.

Working throughout the winter of 1910-11, and for many seasons before and after that, Klovdahl and his workers finally completed the eight bronze gates and 7 to 9 foot tunnel in 1914. The tunnel connected Waldo Lake to the Black Creek drainage and was capable of lowering the level of Waldo Lake by 20 feet.

But the dam was never used. In 1915, public protests forced the Department of Interior to revoke the water withdrawal permit. The dam closed down. In 1960, the Forest Service sealed the gates with concrete to stop leakage. Today, the site is eligible property to the National Register of Historic Places.

It is fortunate that the project failed. Recent evidence has shown that if Waldo Lake had been lowered by 20 feet just once, it would have taken 10 to 20 years to refill. Fashioned like a sieve, the Waldo Basin loses much of its annual precipitation through the porous volcanic rock.

Anglers will find the 420-foot deep lake stocked with eastern brook and rainbow trout. Also, wild kokanee inhabit the waters of this 6,420-acre lake.

Several spur trails lead to campsites near Klovdahl Bay, all situated away from the lake. The South Waldo Shelter sits about 2.0 miles south on the Waldo Lake Trail.

Klovdahl Bay at Waldo Lake

New Shale Ridge Trail

40 SHALE RIDGE TRAIL

Distance: 6.3 miles (one-way)
Elevation gain: 1,800 feet; loss 200 feet
High point: 4,600 feet
Usually open: April through November
Topographic map: The Waldo Lake Area Map
Obtain map from: Willamette National Forest

Variety awaits those willing to climb the steep Shale Ridge Trail. In fact, you probably won't find more variety on any other trail in all of the Waldo Lake Wilderness. Hike through dense vegetation, through dark forests where fallen trees litter the ground. Walk past a stand of ancient cedar trees, some pushing 800 years old. Ford the North Fork Willamette River, then climb the steep trail to the top of Shale Ridge.

Because the first couple miles of trail lead along fairly level ground, this hike (the first 2.5 miles anyway) is perfect for families out for a day hike and should provide solitude as well.

The trailhead can be reached by driving from Westfir (located just north of Oakridge off Oregon Highway 58), and traveling north on North Fork Road No. 19, a paved road, for 30 miles.

Please sign in at the registration box located at the trailhead, then enter the wilderness in 100 yards. Hike Shale Ridge Trail No. 3567 through old-growth forest, following an old road past giant Douglas fir, cedar, and other tree species, including maple trees. Reach Skookum Creek at 1.7 miles.

Cross Skookum Creek and reach a camp 0.1 mile south of the creek. As you continue, you'll see huge western red cedar trees, some nearly 800 years old. The massive old trees bear cones that seem small (1/2-inch) for such a big tree. (For more information on cedar trees, please see the INTRODUCTION TO THE WALDO LAKE WILDERNESS.)

Hike past the reddish giants to 2.5 miles and ford a creek. Next begin a series of several channel crossings as you ford the North Fork Willamette River. When we made our river crossings there were logs leading across all the deep, swift sections. The North Fork can be dangerous at times. Use care when crossing the logs as they can be quite slippery.

The trail would be difficult to follow in this section but signs marked "trail" point the way. Red ribbons mark the trail as well. Reach the west side of the river at 2.7 miles.

Moss covers nearly everything at this point along the trail, providing great opportunities for photos and observation. Anglers can try fishing the river but the Forest Service reports the fish are small and says there is better fishing at the lakes above. (See #22 ERMA BELL LAKES/WILLIAMS LAKE under the listing for trails in the Three Sisters Wilderness for information on these lakes.)

Hiking becomes a bit more difficult at this point. Climb a short, steep section for 0.1 mile to a sign "Vista." This 0.1 trail heads off to the right and climbs at a steep angle to a bluff where a waterfall is visible. The waterfall is located across the river and isn't close enough for photography.

For the next 0.9 mile the trail leads next to or just up the slope from the river, providing good views into the rushing rapids. The trail leads up and down through dense vegetation, with countless numbers of plant life visible. At 3.7 miles switchback up and away from the river. Now the hard part begins!

Climb at a steep angle across the side of Shale Ridge, leveling off at times, then climbing again at a steep rate. At 5.0 miles there are a couple of rock outcrops where one can get a good view into the North Fork Willamette River drainage. Please note, however, it's impossible to actually see the river from this point.

Continue up through hemlock and assorted other tree species before reaching a high point at 5.8 miles. From here it's a gradual downhill to the junction of Blair Lake Trail at 6.3 miles.

41 SIX LAKES/ RIGDON LAKES LOOP

Distance: 18.0 miles (complete loop)
Elevation gain: 1,700 feet; loss 1,700 feet
High point: 5,500 feet
Usually open: July through October
Topographic map: The Waldo Lake Area Map
Obtain map from: Willamette National Forest

The following loop leads past or provides access to 15 lakes (including Waldo Lake), as well as numerous small ponds and unnamed lakes. There are excellent opportunities for fishing in most of the lakes. But hikers beware: crowds fill the trails, especially on holidays and weekends. Hike during the middle of the week if you are looking for peace and quiet.

To reach the trailhead, drive 24 miles southeast from Oakridge, via Oregon Hwy. 58. Turn left on paved Waldo Lake Road No. 5897 and drive another 11.1 miles to a fork in the road. Stay left, now driving paved FS Road No. 5898 for an additional 1.9 miles to a junction. Turn right on paved FS Road No. 515 and follow the sign to the North Waldo Boat and Swim Area. As you near the lake, loop to the right and park in the large parking area near the trailhead, 0.6 mile from the junction.

Pines and firs shade all the loop, with hemlock and western white pine shading the first portion of the trail. There are numerous huckleberry bushes that, when berries are ripe, make a perfect additive for morning pancakes. Bear grass covers much of the ground as well.

Hike Waldo Lake Trail No. 3590 at a gradual up and down grade to 1.6 miles and a junction. Pass several ponds along the way. Catch a glimpse of Waldo Lake off and on through the trees.

The junction leads right to Rigdon Lakes (the return trail) and straight towards Six Lakes. Continue, passing more ponds and a chance for a closeup view of Waldo Lake at 2.2 miles. There's a short spur trail leading to the crystal clear lake.

Rhododendrons line much of the trail now as you hike to a junction and the North Fork Willamette River at 2.9 miles. To the right there is the Wahanna Trail, and to the left a trail leads past the gauging station to Dam Camp just 0.1 mile away.

Head across the bridge to 3.0 miles and another junction. The Waldo Lake Trail continues to the left. Follow the trail to the right, now hiking the Wahanna Trail No. 3583. Enter the wilderness and descend gradually to 3.2 miles and still another junction. Stay straight on the Six Lakes Trail No. 3597 (sign reads "Blair Lake Trail - 5 1/2 miles"). Hike through dense vegetation to a fishing trail at 4.3 miles. The trail leads a short distance to Round Lake.

The Forest Service reports that campsites are few at Round Lake. Most people camp near the Eddeeleo Lakes and hike down to 22 acre Round Lake to fish for both rainbow and brook trout.

Back on the main trail, head to a spur trail leading to Upper Eddeeleo Lake at 4.6 miles. For the next 0.4 mile you'll see several trails leading to potential campsites. Some are difficult to hike because of dense rhododendrons, and a couple of the sites are too close to the water.

At 24 acres, Upper Eddeeleo Lake is the smallest of the two Eddeeleo Lakes, but provides good fishing for brook trout.

Hike up and down at a gradual grade, then cross a bridge at 5.4 miles. Continue to 5.7 miles and a view of Lower Eddeeleo Lake off to the right. Steep terrain surrounds the 160 acre lake, but the Forest Service reports there are a few campsites available. Anglers may hook both brook and rainbow trout.

The trail continues at the same grade, heading through the trees to Long Lake at 7.0 miles. Again the terrain surrounding the lake is steep and the vegetation dense, but there is a spur trail leading to a camp at 7.6 miles. Although the camp is located too close to the lake, it appears to be the only available camp in the area. The Forest Service still allows its use, but may rope it off eventually should a restoration program be enforced. Anglers will find cutthroat and brown trout living in the 50 acre lake.

Additional campsites are available at Upper Quinn Lake. Continue to the 7.9 miles mark and the Upper Quinn Lake Trail No. 3597A. This 1/4-mile trail heads to the left and up to the lake. The trail then skirts along 100 yards of the east shore, providing access to a variety of campsites.

As evidenced by all the sites, this area gets a lot of use, some of it by those who have no respect for the wilderness. Toilet paper littered the ground when we visited the area. Before reaching the lake, we spoke with one of the wilderness rangers. She apologized for any mess we might find at Upper Quinn Lake, stating that she hadn't had the time to clean it up. It's unfortunate that someone has to hike out to these pristine lakes to clean up someone else's toilet paper and other garbage. Please, let's clean up after ourselves. Leave a clean camp for the next wilderness visitor.

The Oregon Department of Fish and Wildlife stocks 20 acre Quinn Lake with brook trout. At 37 feet deep it's good for swimming as well.

Next, hike to the Blair Lake Trail No. 3553 at 8.7 miles. Turn right and descend moderately to 9.1 miles and the Moolack Trail. Moolack is a small, but popular lake, stocked with brook trout. Hike 0.3 miles down the trail to Moolack Lake.

Continue down via the Blair Lake Trail to the Shale Ridge Trail No. 3567 at 9.5 miles. Head right towards Taylor Burn and descend at a moderate to steep grade.

Begin crossing the North Fork Willamette River at 9.9 miles. There are three channels to cross: the west, middle, and east, with campsites located between the three. Logs make fording all the trenchs a bit easier.

From the river, hike up at a steep grade crossing Iva Creek at 10.1 miles and Root Creek at 10.3 miles. Hike through cedar, hemlock, and rhododendrons, with ferns gracing the landscape as you head up the slope.

The vegetation turns to lodgepole and western white pines farther up the slope and then to mixed conifer at 11.7 miles. The Taylor Burn Campground is free, with pit toilets, fire grates, and picnic tables for your convenience. Fresh spring water is also an added plus.

To reach the spring, hike 100 yards down the campground road to your left. At this point notice all the rocks on the left side of the road. Hike over the rocks to the spring, 75 feet from the road. A pipe delivers cold, delicious water.

To continue the loop, head back to the point where you first entered the campground. Remain on the campground road and follow it 200 feet to the Wahanna Trail No. 3583.

It's a gradual up and down for the rest of the loop, with the vegetation growing more lush as you draw nearer to Wahanna Lake. Huckleberries seem to be everywhere.

Pass the trail to East Brook Lake at 11.9 miles. This trail leads 0.5 mile to the lake where brook trout fishing is reported "fair." Continue to Emma Lake at 12.2 miles. Just 4 acres in size, Emma Lake is also stocked with brook trout.

Reach the Whig and Torrey Trail junction at 13.0 miles. The loop continues straight ahead, but those wanting a nice place to camp should turn left at the junction and hike 0.1 mile to Wahanna Lake.

There are several restoration sites located near the lake's shore (please do not camp here), but there are other sites available for camping. Most have obvious spur trails leading to them and are not difficult to find. Wahanna Lake spans 60 acres and provides good fishing opportunities for the angler. The lake is stocked with rainbow trout and at 16 feet deep, is also great for swimming.

Head back to the Wahanna Trail and turn left to continue the loop. Reach another spur trail leading to Wahanna Lake at 13.2 miles. Farther on, come to Lake Kiwa at 14.1 miles. There are several campsites at this pretty lake and good fishing for rainbow and brook trout as well. Rigdon Butte provides a nice backdrop to the 40 acre lake.

At 14.4 miles reach the junction to Rigdon Lakes Trail No. 3555 which also provides access to the Waldo Lake Trail. Turn left and reach Lower Rigdon Lake at 15.0 miles, Upper Rigdon Lake at 15.5 miles. Both of the Rigdon Lakes span 50 acres and both are rated "fair" in the fishing department. At the Lower lake you'll find rainbow trout. Brook trout live in the Upper lake. There are several campsites at both lakes and good swimming opportunities at both as well.

Travel a series of gradual ups and downs to a secondary trail leading to another lake at 16.2 miles. Perhaps this would be a good place to camp if the other lakes are crowded. Reach the Waldo Lake Trail junction at 16.4 miles. Turn left and head back to the trailhead to complete the loop at 18.0 miles.

Golden-Mantled Squirrel

Lake Kiwa

ACKNOWLEDGEMENTS

Along with the many blessings that I receive and thank God for daily (a loving and supportive family, good friends, a roof over my head, and food on the table), I also thank Him for the opportunity to write and photograph, and for my summers spent backpacking.

Here, in God's Wilderness, I inhale the sweet smell of the earth after a spring rain. I hear bull elk bugling, an eerie sound, like a lone whistle in the night. I see deer bouncing through the forest, pikas playing on boulders, eagles soaring in the heavens. I feel the shallow warmth of the sun after the bitter cold of a late summer snowstorm. I feel hordes of mosquitoes sucking my blood. I thank God for all of this (except the mosquitoes).

Roger Aitkenhead, my husband and partner, but most of all my friend, shares all of these experiences with me. Together we swat bothersome bugs, climb mountains, watch eagles soar. Together we struggle to reach our dream. Thank you, Roger.

Sam, our Samoyed, joins us on every journey. Carrying a backpack of his own, he is never a burden, always a joy.

A special thanks must go to my Mom, Beverly Ikenberry. Although she doesn't join us on our backpacking trips, always she is with us. Mom, thank you for being the sweet person who you are. To be your best friend, as well as your daughter, is a gift that I will always treasure.

I am also thankful for the men in my family. To my Dad, Don Ikenberry, and my two brothers, Don and Dave Ikenberry, thank you for believing in me always.

I owe a big "thank-you" to all of my friends, including my dearest friend, Lorraine Miller. Lorraine, and her late husband and our dearly missed friend, Hoss, have blessed us with their friendship for many years now. To my other special friends, I thank you for your love and support.

Many government agencies provided an array of information while working on this book. To all the Forest Service employees who so patiently answered all of my questions, mailed maps and management plans, and even made phone calls for us, thank you. Also, I am grateful to the Oregon Department of Fish and Wildlife and the Bureau of Land Management for sending out prompt replies to my many questions.

Stephanie Hakanson, Aspenwood Studios, has printed hundreds of our negatives, always showing an extraordinary amount of professionalism in the 8X10 black and white photographs she prints for us.

And last (but never least), I would like to express my deep felt gratitude and appreciation for Oral Bullard, my publisher.

Sam and friends

Cover photos: *Rock Creek*
Diamond View Lake
Mt. Washington Wilderness